MexWX

Mexico Weather for Boaters

Second Edition

Captain John E. Rains

Point **L**oma **P**ublishing

Post Office Box 60190
San Diego, CA 92166
(888) 302-BOAT

ISBN 0-9638470-1-5

About the illustrations: The illustrations in this book are designed to be used as educational tools and for travel-planning purposes; they are expressly not to be used for navigation.

About the text: The brief text in this book has been carefully prepared, based on personal experience, official publications and other data deemed reliable, with the purpose of making the experience of pleasure boating more enjoyable.

About the reader's use of the book: All information and directions in this book must be checked against the skipper's own observations and any current official publications pertaining to weather and locale. Every skipper alone is responsible for the safety of his or her crew and vessel, and he or she must plot the safe course. Therefore both the author and publisher specifically disclaim any and all personal liability for loss or risk, to persons or property or both, which might occur either directly or indirectly from any person's use or interpretation of any information in this book. No publication can substitute for good sea sense.

ACKNOWLEDGEMENTS

Thanks to Capitán de Altura Carlos Murillo of the Instituto Oceanografico in Manzanillo for giving me a deeper insight to marine weather in Mexico and especially the Sea of Cortez and Gulf of Tehuantepec.

Thanks to the Port Captains of Ensenada, Cabo San Lucas, Guaymas, Mazatlan, Puerto Vallarta, Manzanillo, Acapulco, Salina Cruz and Puerto Madero for their enlightening discussions with me about weather characteristics in their jurisdictions, and also for their many interesting sea stories.

Thanks to Paul Leverenz, Map Librarian of Scripps Institute of Oceanography, La Jolla, for access to his extensive collection of charts.

Thanks to my wife, Patricia Miller-Rains, for sticking with me through rain and shine, from research through final production.

TO CONTACT AUTHOR
Captain John E. Rains
Rains Yacht Delivery Service
P.O. Box 81669
San Diego, CA 92138
(858) 565-1384
http://home.san.rr.com/caprains

MexWX
Mexico Weather for Boaters

Ensenada

USA

Turtle Bay

Guaymas

Sea of Cortez

Mazatlan

Cabo San Lucas

GULF OF MEXICO

Puerto Vallarta

Cabo Corrientes

Manzanillo

MEXICO

Zihuatanejo

Tehuantepec

Acapulco

Pto. Angel

Pto. Madero

Pacific

**This concise book covers WEATHER encountered by Boaters
traveling along Mexico's entire Pacific Coast
from the U.S. to the Guatemalan border,
including the Sea of Cortez and offshore passage routes between
Baja California and the Mexican mainland.**

MexWX   List of Graphics and Illustrations

Table of Contents

MexWX: Mexico Weather for Boaters

Table of Contents

Table of Contents

Dedicated to...

...all my fellow mariners, novices and veterans alike, who have found their way into Mexico's warmer waters. No matter if you visit there for a short cruise or plan your grand retirement under the sun, I hope my expanded 2nd edition of MexWX serves you well.

Capt. John E. Rains

What the Heck is MexWX?

ᴜᴜᴜᴜᴜᴜᴜᴜᴜᴜᴜᴜᴜᴜᴜᴜᴜᴜᴜᴜᴜᴜᴜᴜᴜᴜᴜᴜᴜᴜ

MexWX is all about Mexico's marine weather on the Pacific side, and it tells boaters how they can use their shipboard radios to know what's going on over the horizon. Sound like a good idea?

MexWX is based on my 20 years of experience while traveling the entire length of Mexico in all seasons, captaining all sizes and kinds of power and sail boats, commercial and yacht, during many dozens of voyages.

Mexico's Pacific coastline measures more than 3,300 miles in length when you include the Sea of Cortez. When traveling from one end to the other, boaters are affected by weather patterns and sea conditions that change drastically from one locale to the next. But because so little solid information has previously been published about marine weather in Mexico, boaters were forced to rely on only a few brief paragraphs in "Sailing Directions."

I studied meteorology in college. I've combined this book-learning with many years of personal experience at sea, observing conditions and predicting weather underway during my own voyages, and, as a consultant, helping other boaters plan their trips. Not to have a good understanding of marine weather, especially in Mexican waters, is like running blind. Will you have head seas or following seas while you push down to Acapulco in January? Will you have wind all the way across the Sea of Cortez, or will it be glassed off for days on end?

The "WX" in MexWX is radio shorthand for "weather." Radio is vital to have onboard where you're going; to shun radio savvy is to play the proverbial ostrich with its head buried in the sand. Radio can't make decisions for you, but it gives you the raw data you need to make your own wise decisions.

When you're hanging out in some beautiful anchorage, radio is your only way to learn that a Screaming Blue Norther is just over the horizon and coming your way. Or that it died off last night. Then you can decide: Is it too late to high-tail it to the next anchorage with better shelter? Or should I stay put and set an extra anchor? Is the coast clear, or is that low-pressure system still lying in wait off Isla Cedros?

Introduction

Radio has long been my other hobby, especially Amateur Radio, and radio is an indispensable part of my daily work in yacht deliveries. Many fellow hams know me better as N6HOY, but I'm always on a different boat, so I'm hard to follow.

I wrote MexWX to fill these two information voids: marine weather in Mexico, and how radio can help you make good decisions.

What's inside MexWX?

In the regular chapters, we'll closely examine the "why" and "how" and "where" and "when" of Mexico's prevailing weather patterns and its infamous Hurricane Season.

➔   How does each weather pattern affect your cruising itinerary? How can you plan your route to take advantage of these patterns?

➔   When and how do Mexican hurricanes form? Where do they move, during which months? What happens when hurricanes jump over land?

➔   Where is it safe to "summer over" and why? What's involved?

The chapter on MexWX Broadcasts talks briefly about minimum equipment and maximum know-how, and then I've described what kind of weather data is available over each of the four types of radios normally found on pleasure boats: VHF, HAM, SSB, and WXFax or weather fax. I've listed all the important stations or services that broadcast data pertaining to specific areas of Mexico's Pacific waters. So that you'll be able to tune into these selected broadcasts, I've listed their frequencies or channels, plus the region from which you can receive each broadcast while on board your boat in Mexican waters.

For the past several years pressure from Congress for budget cuts threatened to permanently axe weather fax radio broadcasts. For the time being, the situation has taken a turn for the better. Weather fax is still being broadcast by radio to mariners at sea. However budget cuts were made affecting the following: NWS staffing was cut from 24 hours a day to 20 hours a day; they dropped the 96-hour forecasts and the longest forecast is now 72 hours; NWS no longer pays for the phone lines to disseminate the charts from their computer data base to the U.S. Coast Guard weather fax stations.

The U.S.C.G. stepped in and provided the funding for the phone lines from their budget so that they could continue broadcasting charts to their own ships at sea. Civilian mariners are the beneficiaries of this largess. Also the U.S.C.G. opened a new weather fax station NMG which covers the Gulf of Mexico and Caribbean to Panama as well as the Pacific coast of Mexico. NMG is a marvelous addition from the stand points of radio propagation and chart coverage.

Then we'll FOCUS on six regions of Pacific Mexico, looking closely at specific conditions you can expect when voyaging in each region: Pacific Baja, inside the Sea of Cortez, along the Gold Coast from the latitudes of Cabo and Puerto Vallarta down to Manzanillo, the southern mainland down to Puerto Angel, the Gulf of Tehuantepec and its infamous gales, even Papagallo winds of Central America.

→ What strange local phenomenon should you be alert for?
→ When is the best time of day, season of the year, to traverse particular parts of each stretch?
→ What if you're approaching Mexico from the south?

In the Appendices, to help you monitor the many Mexican radio broadcasts, we've listed the Spanish meteorological terms you'll hear over the local radio and in the Port Captains' offices when discussing marine weather. The Beaufort Scale will become a second-nature reference, as will the Equivalent Measures appendix. The Bibliography is a bookshelf checklist, and it includes some important meteorological publications you should have onboard when cruising Pacific Mexico.

I hope you'll read through MexWX before you head south, but then keep it in your chart table or near your radio rig for quick reference while you're down here enjoying your boat in Mexico.

Que tenga siempre viento de popa.
Fair winds.

Introduction

Chapter 1

Prevailing Patterns

To understand Mexico's prevailing weather patterns, look at the earth's general air flow to see what causes these seasonal variations.

You knew all this stuff in high school, but in case that's been awhile, here's a brief refresher: At the Equator, which is the hottest region on earth, air heated by the overhead equatorial sun becomes less dense and therefore rises. Rising air creates patches of low pressure, which are nearly permanent features along the Equator. As this air rises it moves toward the poles, begins to cool and therefore becomes more dense. The cooling air begins to sink back to earth, so wherever it sinks it causes areas of high pressure.

Since air always moves from high pressure toward low pressure, we find it at the surface returning toward the Equator. In our northern hemisphere, the direction of these returning surface winds is deflected to the westward due to the Coriolis Effect.

Figure 1 is the over-simplified diagram of air circulation above the rotating earth. In reality, the patterns are

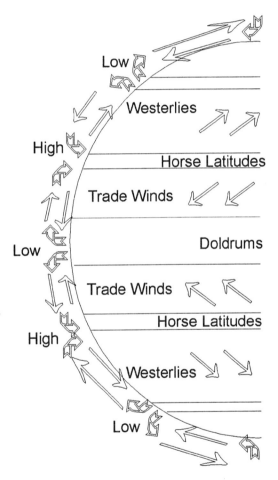

Fig. 1. Mexico's weather encompasses Westerlies, Horse Latitudes, Trade Winds and Doldrums due to seasonal shifting.

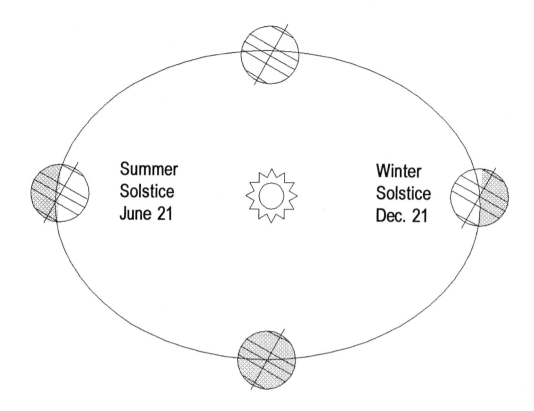

Fig. 2. In the northern hemisphere the sun is directly overhead at the Summer Solstice.

altered by seasonal changes, and eddies and back-eddies are stirred up by the many effects of land masses. The result is a complex, ever-changing movement of air about the earth.

The change of seasons is caused by the 23.5° inclination of the earth's axis to the plane of it's orbit around the sun. As seen in Figure 2, the sun is more directly overhead on the summer solstice (June 21) in the northern hemisphere than it is at winter solstice (Dec. 21) in the same location. Not only are the sun's rays more concentrated during the summer (Fig. 3), but the sun is above the horizon longer; therefore summer is warmer. In winter, the rays of the sun are less concentrated and the number of hours of solar radiation are fewer; consequently winter is cooler.

Mexico's Pacific coast is affected by seasonal movements and also by the daily interaction of these wind belts: the Doldrums, Trade Winds, Horse Latitudes, Westerlies.

Doldrums — Also known as the Inter-Tropical Convergence Zone (ITCZ), this belt of low pressure lies near the Equator. It is an area of light and variable winds, much cloudiness and heavy rain showers. During the northern-hemisphere summer the ITCZ moves northward following the maximum heating of the overhead sun where it affects the Mexican Coast. This annual movement accounts for Mexico's two distinct seasons — wet (when the ITCZ is present on the coast) and dry (when the ITCZ has moved closer to the Equator). These seasons are sometimes jokingly called "mud" and "dust."

The Trade Winds — These winds blow outward from the high pressure zones near 30°N and 30°S toward the low pressure of the ITCZ. In the northern hemisphere this north-to-south flow is deflected toward the west (Coriolis Effect), generally making winds blow from the northeast. The Trade Winds are more constant than other winds on earth, especially over the open ocean. Although most of the Mexican Pacific coast lies in this belt, the very high mountains of Mexico effectively block the Trades in Pacific coastal waters; they aren't usually felt until you're hundreds of miles offshore. Farther south, however, in the Gulf of Papagallo off Costa Rica, the Trade Winds can cross the Central American continent at a low spot and then blow strongly into the Pacific.

The Horse Latitudes — North of the Trade Winds we find a belt of high pressure caused by air that has flowed northward from the Doldrums in the upper atmosphere, then it has cooled and descended to the surface. Horse Latitudes are

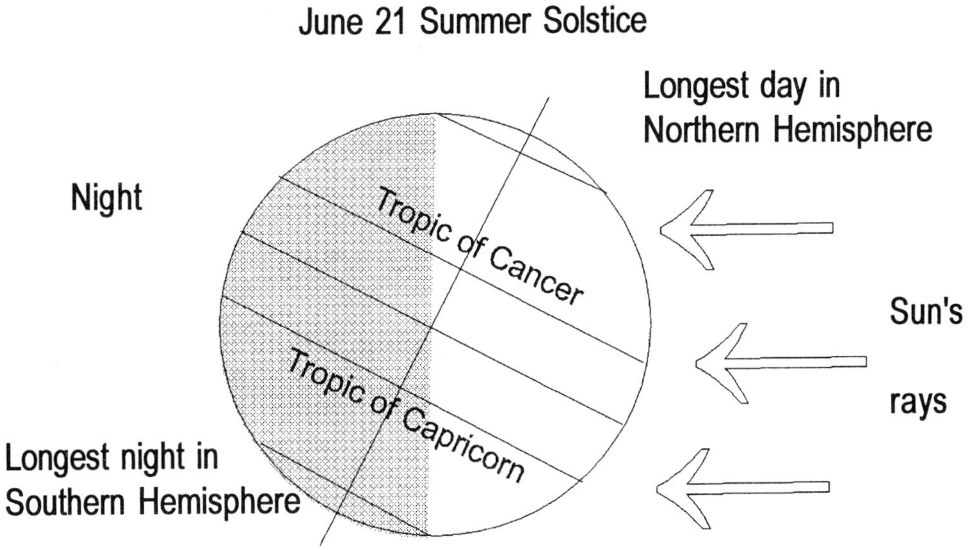

June 21 Summer Solstice

Longest day in
Northern Hemisphere

Night

Tropic of Cancer

Sun's

rays

Tropic of Capricorn

Longest night in
Southern Hemisphere

Fig. 3. The sun is directly over Cabo San Lucas on the Tropic of Cancer on June 21.

marked by dry air and light wind. (This air belt got it's name in the Atlantic when sailing ships ran out of wind, then ran out of water. Sadly, their cargoes of horses died of thirst and were cast overboard. Hense, the Horse Latitudes.)

The Pacific High, which rides between California and Hawaii, floats on the Horse Latitudes, and the terms are sometimes interchanged. The Pacific High affects northwestern Mexico at times as far south as Manzanillo. Seasonally the high moves north and south with the sun. Depending on the position of this high, it can make strong northwesterlies if you're well off the Baja coast, or, if the high moves near the Baja coast, expect light and variable winds close in. In winter the Pacific High sometimes moves inland over the western U.S. and causes Screaming Blue Northers in the Sea of Cortez.

The Westerlies — When the Pacific High is well established in the spring and summer, the Westerlies (really northwesterlies at this point) blow quite boisterously along the Baja coast and even to the Mexican mainland.

El Niño

El Niño is an unusual pool of warm water that forms off the coast of Peru every few years. The '97-98 El Niño Southern Oscillation has grown extremely large and drifted westward into the Pacific where it dampens normal Trade Winds and disrupts ocean currents, creating abnormal weather patterns on the global scale. The '82-83 El Niño brought devastating coastal storms to California—but droughts to Peru, Australia and Indonesia.

"Should you go to Mexico in an El Niño season?" YES, BUT...

→ Know how to monitor the weather, and be extra vigilant about doing so daily.
→ Don't go out in bad weather; put into port if it looks like it's going to turn bad.
→ Don't be in a hurry to meet deadlines that tempt you out into bad weather.

During a normal cruising season, Mexico's weather is so benign that many cruisers go merrily along without knowing how to monitor the weather, and they used to get away with it. However, in an El Niño year you, that would be foolish.

Every El Niño year is different, so it's impossible to predict this one. But based on past performance, here are three possibilities:

1. A more active Mexican hurricane season: We've already had more violent storms more frequently, and they have a propensity to curve and hit the mainland. By January 1, I wouldn't expect any tropical weather in Mexico, but I'll still remain on the lookout for anything unusual. Also, hurricane season may begin as early as May 1 instead of the last week of May. Either return home by then, or – if you're summering over – move up into the Sea of Cortez by then and find yourself a safe hidey-hole.

2. Stronger and longer coastal storms in California: The '82-83 El Niño gales off California reached far down the Baja peninsula, so the Sea of Cortez could experience stronger than normal Northers that come in on the back sides of the low pressure systems that cause California's gales. Be extra cautious in Baja. In fact, a good plan would be to spend the winter months over on the mainland, anywhere from Puerto Vallarta south, which has the most benign weather of the season. Then move back into the Sea of Cortez in the late spring when the winds should be lighter and warmer.

3. Lighter than normal spring Northwesterlies along outer Baja: This was a great advantage during past El Niños, making the return trip from Mexico much more pleasant.

Prevailing Patterns

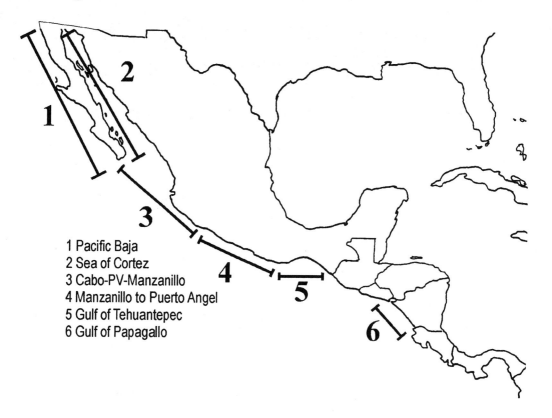

1 Pacific Baja
2 Sea of Cortez
3 Cabo-PV-Manzanillo
4 Manzanillo to Puerto Angel
5 Gulf of Tehuantepec
6 Gulf of Papagallo

Fig. 4 .   These six geograhic regions are the
FOCUS areas of the following six chapters.

Chapter 2

Focus: Pacific Baja

∿∿∿∿∿∿∿∿∿∿∿∿∿∿∿∿∿∿∿∿

Because Baja California is adjacent to Southern California, many aspects of its weather are similar. Prevailing winds are from the northwest, moderated by the influence of land-sea breezes near the shore. Fog and overcast are common. Well off shore (60 plus miles) the wind is often out of the northwest at a constant 20 knots or more throughout the day and night. As you travel farther south the wind, fog and overcast diminish regardless of the time of year.

Air temperatures are remarkably cool along this "outside" coastline in all but the late summer. Not until you round the tip of Baja at Cabo Falso on the approach to Cabo San Lucas do you enter a tropical regime. This change is quite dramatic. However even Cabo has its cool-winter years.

WINTER

Winter along the Pacific coast of Baja brings occasional stormy weather. This is caused by a southward shift of the Jet Stream and a corresponding breakdown of the Pacific High. The Pacific High is quasi-stationary between Hawaii and the U.S. mainland during spring and summer. Cold fronts invade during winter. (Fig. 5) The strongest fronts are preceded by southeast gales and rain, followed by winds shifting to the northwest, and finally by clearing. The frequency of southeast gales diminishes farther south along the Baja coast, rarely reaching the mid to southern sections of Baja. But they can happen.

The first of February we were southbound and 24 hours out of San Diego on "Heddy," a 112-foot Baltic ketch. Weather reports showed gale warnings for southerly winds in 24 hours. What rotten luck. We thought we were off on a downhill slide to Paradise and instead we were going to buck gale-force head winds.

What to do? Protection from southerlies is hard to come by on the coast of Baja. We were only about 20 miles from Isla San Martin. A sand spit on the southeast corner of the island was the only good protection in southerlies, so we headed that way.

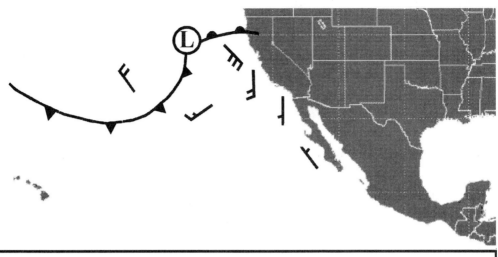

	Examples	Explanation of wind arrows
⇝	30 knots from SE	Arrows fly with the wind.
⇂	20 knots from NW	Each feather signifies 10 knots.
↙	15 knots from SW	Each half feather signifies 5 knots.
⇂	5 knots from NW	A triangle signifies 50 knots. Avoid areas with triangles.

Fig. 5. Winter Cold Front threatens to invade Baja; light winds are in advance.

We anchored in the lee of the spit along with several fishing boats and a kelp cutter out of Ensenada. For two days we stood 24-hour anchor watch, while 35-knot southerlies raked us and huge waves broke on the little sand spit. Other vessels dragged, but we held. Finally the wind dropped and hauled around to its normal northwesterly, so we shoved off.

Northbound sailors might take heart from this story, watching for a tail wind to help them up Baja. I must add that in 100 some trips along the Baja coast in all seasons, that was the only southerly I encountered while in a sailboat.

More often, the winter breakdown in the Pacific High causes an interruption in the usually strong northwesterly flow. Several days before an approaching cold front, the wind may switch from its customary northwest direction or more often become light and variable. This condition may last for days, especially if the cold front stalls out farther to the north.

When this happens, southbound sailors are singing the blues and whistling for wind. They could head well off shore where the wind should be steadier and not influenced by diurnal fluctuations of the land-sea breeze. Unfortunately, the wind may be flat calm well off shore as well.

This calm pattern makes for great northbound passages, even with sailboats, when the best one could hope for is not having wind on the nose and having to motor. We have made several fast, comfortable power boat passages from Cabo to San Diego during November and December. The fastest took 30 hours. The seas were flat calm and we never even got spray on the windshield.

After the passage of a winter low-pressure system, high pressure often moves into the inter-mountain basin near Nevada. (Fig. 8) This generates a north to east offshore wind known in Southern California as a "Santa Ana." Such winds blow most strongly near shore and especially down the canyon mouths. Though they can reach dangerous strengths in Southern California, they rarely do so in Baja. Sometimes a Santa Ana can help on a northbound trip, as in the following example.

We flew down to La Paz on the first of December to pick up a 60-foot schooner to bring back to San Diego. During our last night at the marina in La Paz the wind picked up from the north. I figured it would, because it had been raining when we left San Diego; 48 hours later the cold front had caught up with us. The first two hours we had a wet ride as we motored northward into the wind and sea, until we began to turn toward the south in the San Lorenzo Channel. Then we began to sail in a 20-knot breeze.

We smoked down the Cerralvo Channel on a broad reach, surfing in eight- to 10-foot seas. This channel runs between Cerralvo Island and the east side of Baja's cape. Especially when wind and tide oppose one another, it generates some notoriously steep seas. They were lofty and close together this time, and the ride was uncomfortable even going downhill. The wind stayed with us till San Jose del Cabo and then died as we got into the lee of the cape mountains. The sea was flat calm as we motored around Cabo Falso.

The morning forecast on the California/Baja Net mentioned strong high pressure building over the inter-mountain plateau of the western U.S., creating a Santa Ana in Southern California. A Norther was still blowing in the Sea of Cortez, and north through east winds were predicted for the outside of Baja. Good news for us. Any break from the normally strong northwesterly flow would allow us to get some drive from our sails and not have to meet those square waves head on.

With that forecast in mind I hugged the shoreline rather than take a straight course to Mag Bay. We had a 10-knot northeast wind on the beam and a flat sea, so we made good time.

At Cabo San Lazaro the morning forecast called for more of the same, northeast winds. I then decided to take a straight shot to Turtle Bay. That turned out to be a tactical error, because at sunset that night, the wind came out of the northwest. We made slow, wet progress for several hours until it lightened and shifted to the north. If I had hugged the coast, I believe I would have had more favorable winds, even though it would have been a longer distance.

Usually I go through the Dewey Channel between Isla Natividad and Punta Eugenia, and then up the eastern side of Cedros Island, which is normally the lee. But since the wind was northeast, no lee would exist. Instead, I went outside Natividad and between Cedros and San Benito.

The area just north of Isla Cedros is something of a "bugaboo" for northbound boats, because the northwesterlies pile up against the 4,000-foot-tall precipice on the island's north end. This time, however, the boogy man was lying in wait for us at the southwest corner of Cedros, at Cabo San Agustin. We struggled against lumpy seas at three knots until finally rounding it. Things lightened up, and at the north end the wind was flat calm.

The forecast called for more of the same, a long-term Santa Ana. A large area of very high pressure, 1038 millibars, had taken up residence over Utah. When we again closed with the coast, we alternated between calms and gusty offshore winds that blew down the canyons and valleys. It was like that the rest of the way into San Diego.

We were lucky! Once again November-December proved to be the best time of the year for a northbound trip. We had ridden the High Pressurelator all the way home.

The area between Mag Bay and Turtle Bay gets easterly Santa Ana-like winds in winter. Typically however a Santa Ana is weak and causes light, cold winds and very good visibility. Occasionally though, easterlies can make for cold, uncomfortable going if not down right dangerous conditions.

During the first week in November one year, we were bringing a 78-foot motoryacht from Puerto Vallarta to San Diego. We had a calm trip until the night we were passing Turtle Bay, when the wind suddenly gusted up very strongly off the beach. Fortunately we were only five miles offshore of Turtle Bay and I turned and headed straight in toward the harbor. It was a wet and uncomfortable five miles, and as we entered the bay we had a surprise. The wind had picked up an enormous amount of sand and was blowing it our way, horizontally, reducing visibility to zero.

I anchored on the east side of the bay, away from town, because I didn't want to have to worry about myself or other vessels dragging anchor. We payed out 7:1 scope and rode comfortably. The wind howled and the anemometer showed 50 knots, as we stood anchor watch throughout the night.

As dawn approached we saw that the white boat was completely caked with dark ocher-colored grit blown down the mountains and off the beach. But the wind hadn't lessened. It was Pat's birthday, so we celebrated by sitting in the pilot house, reading books, writing articles, and playing cards, all the while trying to hear radio weather reports through the shriek of the wind.

During the afternoon the wind began to drop, and toward sunset we were able to hose down the dirty boat. The wind had dropped significantly by evening so we departed. Though a lumpy sea was left over, it continued to go down and we had a good trip the rest of the way to San Diego.

SPRING

As the seasons progress, the frequency of invading low-pressure systems drops. May is when most cruisers return from Mexico, before the beginning of hurricane season. By then, the Pacific High is a seasonally permanent feature between Hawaii and the continent. Likewise, a thermal trough of low pressure has developed over Yuma, Arizona, caused by heating in the deserts. The clockwise rotation of wind around the high and the pressure differential between it and the Yuma Low makes the wind strong and steady out of the northwest along the Baja coast. (Fig. 6)

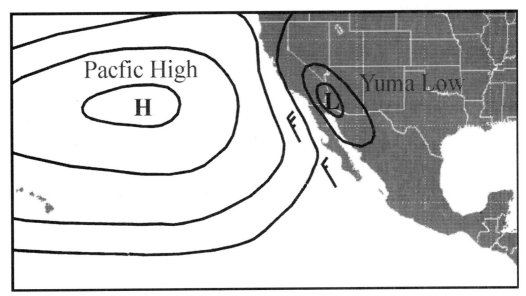

Fig. 6. Springtime conditions create strong northwesterly winds and a wet ride home.

Consequently, spring can be the most difficult time to head north.

We've made sailing trips south during May, delivering boats for Mexican clients. Several times we've made the run from San Diego to Cabo San Lucas in four and a half days — not bad for vessels in the 40- to 45-foot range. In one case we made 400 miles in two days, surfing down huge waves, white knuckles firmly gripping the helm, afraid to look over our shoulders at the white-crested monsters that kept trying to crawl over the transom and into the cockpit.

Here's what usually occurs. A daily (diurnal) cycle of wind occurs along this shoreline and is caused by the sun. The wind is light or calm from sunset until late morning, when the wind builds up, stays up through the afternoon, and then dies at sunset. The air over the land heats up from the sun during the day and then cools off rapidly at night. The air over the ocean, however, remains at a much more constant temperature. During the heat of the day the air over the land actually rises. As it rises it draws in the cooler air from the ocean. This generates the seabreeze, which peaks in mid-afternoon and dies near sunset. (Fig. 7)

At night, the land cools off rapidly, and the cooling air sinks downward and blows out toward your boat offshore. This is the land breeze, and its effect on you diminishes with your distance from the shoreline. A land breeze peaks just before sunrise and is much weaker than the seabreeze, rarely more than 10 knots; often it is non-existent. If nothing else is affecting the weather, that means a calm night.

If you're northbound in late spring, you can take advantage of the land-sea breeze cycle close to shore. Stay near shore during the calm night and morning hours, and then tack offshore in the afternoon when the wind is strongest, especially around headlands. You could also plan to drop the hook in a protected anchorage, rest during the period of strongest winds, and then put to sea after sundown

This is contrary to the way most seaman like to do things. They tend to head offshore at night to get away from any unseen hard things associated with land. Traveling inshore all night requires much more precise navigation, a good radar, sharp eyes, and that thermos of strong coffee. Obviously power boats will have a better chance to complete the run between distant anchorages before the wind comes up, but sail cruisers who know all the gunk holes can use the same tactic.

The main point to remember when heading north is to keep moving if the weather is calm. Some inexperienced cruisers like to travel for a day, then spend several days resting, and then travel for another day. This is fine; it's what people go cruising for — rest and relaxation. However along the coast of Baja, good traveling weather going north is very rare. You should take advantage of it by pushing on. Otherwise you'll exhaust yourself by trying to move when it's too windy and then waste the calm periods trying to recuperate. That's when you take forever to get home.

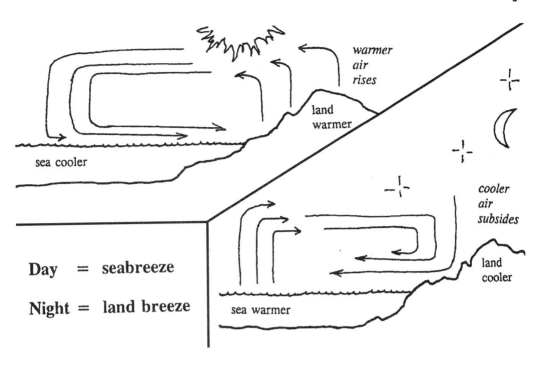

Day = seabreeze

Night = land breeze

Fig. 7. Headed north you can use the land-sea breeze cycle to your advantage.

November 1 marks the official end of hurricane season in Mexico and thus the beginning of the Mexican cruising season, which lasts until June 1. Thus, one traditional itinerary calls for heading down in November and returning north in May. First-timers don't realize that the prevailing northwesterly wind along Baja is at its lightest in November, just when they need it most to head south. And May is rough coming north; the northwesterly is strongest when most of them return in May, making for a very rough return trip.

In planning your first trip to Mexico you can use this knowledge (light winds in November, strong winds in May) to your advantage. Too much wind on the nose is worse than light winds at your back, so plan for it.

A better one-year itinerary is to head south in November, summer over in the northern Sea of Cortez (to avoid hurricanes) and return to the states the following November after hurricane season. This same route can be covered in six months if you go south in May, summer over, and return north in November. We think a Mexican dream cruise deserves more time than that, but it can be done.

The possibilities are many; just remember that November and December are the easiest months in which to head north.

Cape Effect

All along the west coast of Baja California, not solely at Cabo San Lucas, existing winds tend to increase around headlands. This is accentuated when the afternoon seabreeze kicks in. Several anchorages in the lee of headlands are notorious for their Cape Effect. As the wind funnels over the particular headland, it lines up with different canyons and gusts strongly down them. The wind usually dies away to calm in the night and early morning hours.

Santo Thomas, just south of Ensenada, is one such anchorage. I was anchored there in my own boat years ago, with my small inflatable trailing off the stern quarter. The wind was quite gusty that afternoon. One very strong gust died as quickly as it came; a couple of minutes later another gust hit us from almost astern. Before the boat could swing on her anchor and line up with the new wind direction, the inflatable blew into our cockpit. Now, that's a violent wind shift.

Other Baja anchorages known for gusty winds are Colnett, San Carlos, Santa Maria and the north end of Cedros.

The entire region of Cabo San Lucas has a huge Cape Effect especially during the late spring. The wind blows from the northwest 20 knots or more in the afternoon, making it nearly impossible to leave Cabo San Lucas northbound. In such conditions, it's best to depart at around 0400 when it's calmest. The wind dies away the more miles you get away from the cape. On some occasions this wind blows day and night for several days.

This Cape Effect has another peculiar characteristic during the spring months. Beginning northwest of Cabo San Lucas it parallels the coastline, bends around the cape and ends up blowing as a southerly in the Sea of Cortez.

I was bringing a 54-foot DeFever trawler back from La Paz in late May. When we left La Paz we had a 20-knot southerly, a head wind, as we plowed down the Cerralvo Channel. The wind remained on the nose as we turned southwest. The wind stayed on the nose we passed Cabo San Lucas, rounded Cabo Falso, and headed northwest. This weather condition is known as Bad Luck.

SUMMER & FALL

Hurricanes generally haven't threatened Baja California waters until August. But there's nothing general about hurricanes when one's heading your way. Their frequency in this region peaks in September, and October is still in jeopardy. Baja's southern regions are most affected. More on Baja's summer weather in the hurricane chapter.

Chapter 3

Focus: Sea of Cortez

Weather phenomena in the Sea of Cortez vary throughout the year, so we'll look at them season by season

WINTER

Prevailing winds during fall and winter in the Sea of Cortez are northwesterly. During the night-through-morning hours, the land breeze is normally calm to light, becoming its strongest at dawn. Then the seabreeze begins and, by mid-afternoon, reaches it's peak. Winds are strongest during winter months when the season's most significant feature is the Norther, not affectionately known as the "Screaming Blue Norther."

Northers

Strong, cold north wind in the winter in the Sea of Cortez often grows to strengths that disrupt navigation for sail and power alike, often for days on end. Northers are caused by conditions similar to those that produce Santa Anas in Southern California.

After the passage of a low-pressure system over the Pacific coast of the U.S., the ocean air that has quickly pushed in behind it then slows down over land because of the increased friction from the terrain. This air

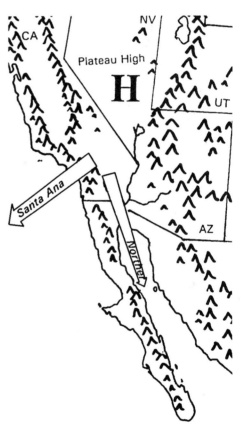

Fig. 8. The Plateau High creates Santa Anas in Southern California and Northers in the Sea of Cortez.

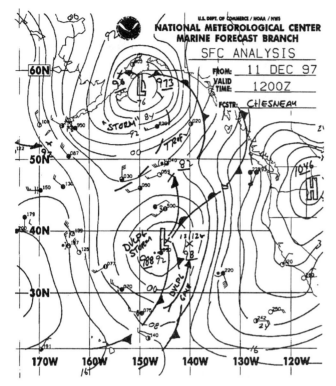

Fig. 9. A strong 1046 mb high over Idaho is causing a Santa Ana in Southern California and a Norther in the Sea of Cortez in this actual surface analysis from NMC.

mass is left stranded in the region east of the Sierra Mountains and west of the Rockies, forming a mound of air. This air accumulation is referred to as the "Plateau High."

The Plateau High disperses by flowing outward just above the land surface toward adjacent areas. Since the air gathers over land that is at least a mile high, it takes the path of least resistance by flowing downward with gravity and seeking low passes toward the sea. In Southern California its effects are felt as a Santa Ana when the path is through the Cajon Pass, into the Santa Ana River Valley, thence back out to sea. (See Figs. 8 and 9.)

When the Plateau High is centered in the eastern part of the plateau, the air also flows southward via the Salton Sea trough and the Colorado River Valley into the Sea of Cortez. The north wind continues to be channeled southward in to the Sea of Cortez between the spine of Baja and the mountains of the Mexican mainland toward overall perennial low pressure near the Equator. Depending on the strength of the High, its effects can be felt the entire length of Baja, though the force of the wind diminishes with distance from the High.

Such strong wind raises a short, steep chop for which the area is notorious. Mariners should stay put if a Norther is blowing or seek shelter if one is predicted.

The Norther carries with it cold air from the Arctic, so winter temperatures in the Sea of Cortez are much cooler than first-time cruisers expect. If you're looking for the kind of cruising where you can get out in the dinghy wearing light clothing, maybe get a little wet and not mind, don't plan to venture north of Puerto Escondido during the winter.

Some hearty souls from Alaska or Siberia hope to make the most of their cruising time, so they lay out an itinerary to visit places like Willard-Gonzaga, Isla Angel la Guardia and Bahia Los Angeles during the winter.

However, it's not until everyone on board has been cooped up below decks for days on end, bundled in every shred of clothing available, even in their bunks at night, with their lips turning blue and snapping irritably at each other... that's when Northers become known as "Screaming Blue Northers." I think the name has as much to do with their emotional effect as with anything meteorological.

Elefantes

In areas where Baja California has terrestrial gaps that cross the peninsula, strong wind on the Pacific can funnel across into the Sea of Cortez. The wind can gust very strongly at the mouths of these low spots. Also, along the ridges these gaps overlooking the Sea of Cortez, Elefantes can occur. Your visual warning just before an Elefante begins is a roiling or tubularly horizontal cloud along the mountainous

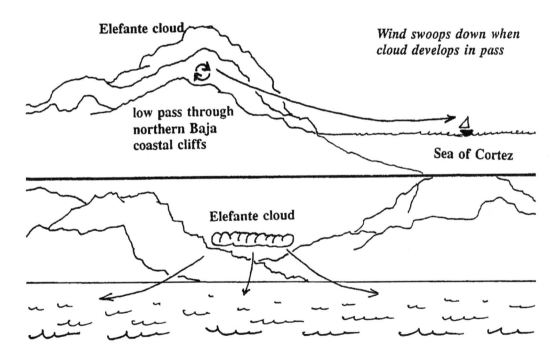

Fig. 10. Rolling clouds above low spots in the terrain show that an Elefante is blowing.

ridge line of the peninsula or along the tops of the cliffs. (Fig. 10) The tubular cloud is not large, and it may move, fade and rebuild. In somebody's imagination, these tubular clouds looked like the trunks of elephants flailing in the air, and thus the local term "Elefante" was originated.

Where and when? Bahia Los Angeles and Gonzaga Bay are most notorious for these winds, and they're most prevalent in the spring. They are generally westerly, but because they're localized winds by nature, they're rarely dangerous to seaworthy vessels, though they could cause a knock-down if you failed to reef fast enough. And close below the mountains, an Elefante can kick up a significant sea.

SUMMER

Long periods of calm dominate the weather in this enclosed body of water throughout the summer, and as air temperatures grow very hot, so too do water temperatures. Fishermen love the warm water, because it draws north the pelagic game fish. Marlin are caught even off San Carlos and Guaymas. Power boaters who have air-conditioning love it. Deck awnings can routinely be set and left up for weeks. Fans below decks are left running as long as possible, long after the air scoops have collapsed.

So sailboats need reliable auxiliaries to get around, because sailing is usually impossible during the summer. The sail inventory should include some very light drifters. When there is enough wind to sail by, to make a move to the next destination, it's normally from the south, particularly in the southern regions.

Why? A semi-permanent area of low pressure sits over Yuma at the head of the Sea of Cortez, caused by intense summer heat over the desert. Wind flows from the south up the axis of the Sea of Cortez to feed into this low.

Use this knowledge to plan your summer itinerary. Many boats coming from the US depart La Paz, gunk hole up the peninsula as far as Puerto Escondido or Santa Rosalia, then cross to San Carlos on the mainland when the tropical southerlies offer them a boost. If you're coming up from southern Mexico before summer, you may get as far as Mazatlan before crossing over to the Baja peninsula, then cross back or continue on toward San Felipe.

El Corumuel

The La Paz area gets a unique, delightful but only occasional summer phenomenon known as the "El Corumuel," a southerly wind that blows at night. When a Corumuel starts, it comes up around sunset and dies after sunrise, conveniently carrying away the excessive heat from muggy summer nights. Wind scoops up.

Corumuels seldom disrupt navigation, but they do make untenable the many anchorages on the east side of Isla Partida and Isla Espiritu Santo. If you're anchored out at these islands when a Corumuel starts up, be ready to get out and head back toward La Paz or elsewhere.

Hurricanes

Hurricanes can strike inside the Sea of Cortez anytime between mid-July and late October, either scooting up the open water between the cape and the Puerto Vallarta area, or crossing over the peninsula and reforming in the Sea of Cortez. More on those in the hurricane section.

Sea of Cortez

Chapter 4

Focus: Cabo to Mexican Mainland

wwwwwwwwwwwwwwwwwwwwwwww

This open-ocean leg between the south tip of the Baja California peninsula and any point on the mainland is often the cruisers' first encounter with an offshore passage. When cruising Mexico, this passage may be your greatest challenge.

CABO TO MAZATLAN, PUERTO VALLARTA AND MANZANILLO

How is it different? During most of the mileage, your vessel is crossing water that is far more affected by broad weather patterns than by the moderating influences of land. High-seas conditions can exist in all but the first and last few miles. And, unlike coastal piloting, there's no shelter to seek at the end of a full day when you've had enough. Although this isn't always a strenuous crossing, it requires some forethought and preparation.

Prevailing winds on this passage generally are northwesterly, so crossing from Cabo to the Manzanillo area puts the wind and swell at your back. In light northwesterlies that have very little sea running with them, this passage can be downwind heaven.

Conversely, during general prevailing northwesterlies, coming from Manzanillo north toward Cabo can be an upwind beat. Again, it's the consistancy of the unmoderated wind strengths and the resulting size of the seas found across this passage that are not like what you grew accustomed to while coastal cruising.

The main weather alert here is for Northers blowing down from the Sea of Cortez. Though their wind intensity decreases the farther south you are, the stronger ones can affect or even cause problems for a vessel making this crossing. Northers are usually more problematic for northbound boats than for southbound boats. Northers rarely reach all the way down to Manzanillo. If the prevailing northwesterlies have turned off, you can still plan to sail across from Cabo to Manzanillo with the boost of the next Norther, but have enough fuel onboard to motor from the time the Norther dies out till you reach the coastal land-sea breezes.

Cabo to Mexican Mainland

Northbound, the weather can kick up on you sometimes. Because of the distances involved you may start off with the "all clear" and get into headwinds out in the middle. In fact the wind increases the closer you get to the cape. On several trips, I have had calm beginnings with the wind picking up to 20 knots or more from the northwest beginning about 100 miles from Cabo San Lucas.

PASSAGE ROUTES

You can choose from three basic routes to the mainland, Fig. 11 below.

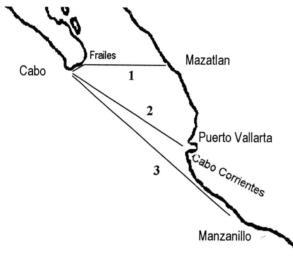

(1.) Cabo to Mazatlan. The shortest route across, 160 miles, is between the anchorages at Punta Los Frailes and Mazatlan. Frailes is 45 miles northwest of Cabo San Lucas in the Sea of Cortez and provides good anchorage in the prevailing northwest to north winds. The north side of Frailes is also decent protection in rare southerlies. It's a great staging area — a place to sit and wait for the right weather conditions for crossing to Mazatlan, or to duck into on the return passage.

Because the Frailes-to-Mazatlan crossing is the most northerly of the three alternatives, it can get the strongest north winds. Your course will be more easterly than the other alternatives.

(2.) Cabo to Puerto Vallarta. This passage is 290 miles of open ocean, and it can be delightful — a southeast course with northwest to north prevailing winds.

The Islas Tres Marias are about 200 miles southeast of Cabo and just slightly north of the rhumb line to Vallarta. They are prison islands, and the Mexican government enforces its prohibition against any vessels coming within 20 miles of them.

Coming back from Puerto Vallarta to Cabo can be tough, because you will have more head winds. You can shorten this crossing by 20 miles by using the anchorage at Punta Mita, right at the northern entrance to Bahia Banderas. Punta

Mita is a large anchorage, well protected from prevailing winds and has good holding ground. If you poke your nose out and find it still too rough, you can turn back easily.

(3.) Cabo to Manzanillo. This route is a serious open-ocean crossing of 400 miles. It's weather and tactics are described in depth above. You can shorten it by 30 miles by jumping off from (or landing on) the mainland at Chamela, a good anchorage in prevailing weather.

Cabo Corrientes Effect

Cabo Corrientes, the major headland west-southwest of Puerto Vallarta, causes northwest afternoon winds to pick up, creating a Cape Effect similar to that found in the approaches to Cabo San Lucas. Cape Effects in general are discussed in the Pacific Baja chapter. The Cabo Corrientes Effect is most frequent and strongest in winter months. Time your northbound passage around Cabo Corrientes so it occurs during the early morning hours.

Cabo to Mexican Mainland

Chapter 5

Focus: Manzanillo to Puerto Angel

ᘉᘉᘉᘉᘉᘉᘉᘉᘉᘉᘉᘉᘉᘉᘉᘉᘉᘉᘉᘉᘉ

Manzanillo, Ixtapa, Zihuatanejo, Acapulco, Puerto Escondido, Puerto Angel and all the beautiful anchorages sprinkled in between are blessed with user-friendly weather during the regular cruising season.

WINTER and SPRING

During the winter/spring cruising season, the 500-mile section of coast from Manzanillo to Puerto Angel (south of Acapulco, at the entrance to the Gulf of Tehuantepec) has the most benign weather in all of Mexico. Average wind strengths are 3 to 12 knots, perfect for relaxed sailing, average temperatures are in the 80s, and the sun shines every day.

Latitude-wise, you're now in the Trade Wind belt, but because the Sierra Madre mountains block this easterly pattern, you won't experience anything like a prevailing wind. It's an area of light variables, and the direction of wind and swell most commonly is from the southwest.

If you're looking for something consistent to plan around, remember the land-sea breeze. Weather and sea conditions here are influenced by this regular phenomenon. (Fig. 7) In the afternoon, winds build to their maximum strength, usually from the southwest, though they won't be as strong as you've experienced farther north. Calm winds often persist for days, particularly the farther south you go.

Beyond Puerto Escondido, the wind can sometimes even come out of the east, depending on what's happening in the Gulf of Tehuantepec.

Terral

In the early morning (peaking at dawn) we get a gentle offshore breeze known to locals as the "Terral." Sailors take advantage of it by staying close to shore, because sometimes it's all the wind there is during the daily cycle.

Manzanillo to Puerto Angel

For years, the San Diego Yacht Club used to sponsor a race from San Diego to Acapulco. During my yacht deliveries that happened to cross this stretch at the same time, I often overheard and talked with race boats. The big topic of conversation was that from Manzanillo south to Acapulco, winds were so light that it turned the race into a drifting contest. About the only wind they could count on was the light morning breezes of the Terral. Eventually, race organizers changed the event's terminus to Manzanillo and sometimes Mazatlan. At least now a greater percentage of the overall route is sailed with a prevailing wind.

SUMMER and FALL

For pleasure boats, this is a very dangerous section of coast to visit during summer and fall hurricane season, because the prevailing wind is south to southwest. Almost all the anchorages and harbors here are wide open to the south and they get ravaged frequently. The possible exceptions — in order of their usefulness — are Lázaro Cárdenas, Marina Ixtapa, Barra Navidad's lagoon if you draw less than six feet, Manzanillo's San Pedrito lagoon, and tiny Papanoa.

If you have to be in this region during hurricane season, read (or memorize) the chapter on hurricanes.

Hot and sunny with light winds is the rule in Acapulco during winter and spring.

Focus: Gulf of Tehuantepec

~~~~~~~~~~~~~~~~~~~~~~~~~~~~~~~~~~~~

Weather in the Gulf of Tehuantepec (tay-WANT-ay-peck) is best described in one word, WINDY. This gulf is adjacent to the Isthmus of Tehuantepec, which is a huge north-south valley running across the narrowest section of Mexico, between two massive mountain ranges. The Isthmus of Tehuantepec was proposed as the site of a trans-oceanic canal, before the building of the Panama Canal through the Isthmus of Panama.

Tehuantepec's geography combines with regional weather patterns to create a frequent gale-force wind infamously known to boaters as a "Tehuantepecker."

Here's how it happens: Intense continental high pressure over Texas causes strong north winds in the Gulf of Mexico. (Fig. 11) Lining up with the valley across

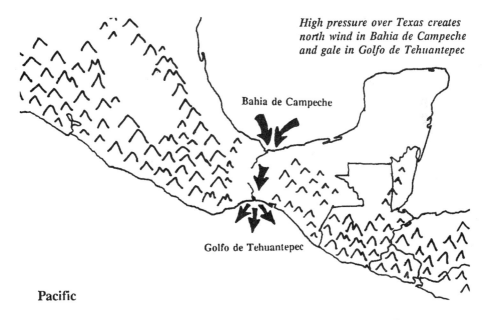

High pressure over Texas creates north wind in Bahia de Campeche and gale in Golfo de Tehuantepec

Bahia de Campeche

Golfo de Tehuantepec

Pacific

Fig. 11. Gale winds blast toward the Equator over the Isthmus of

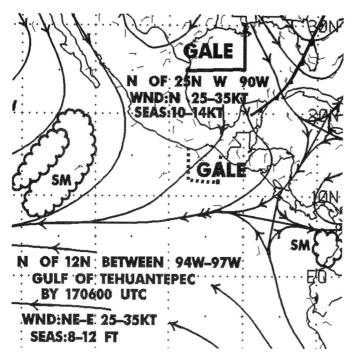

Fig. 12. A boundary drawn around the perimeter of the gale in the Gulf of Tehuantepec shows that trying to go outside of it means going an enormous distance out of the way. Running close to shore is shorter and avoids high seas allowed by fetch.

the Isthmus of Tehuantepec and, in a potent venturi effect, they intensify and sweep out into the Pacific hundreds of miles, as they flow toward the perennial low pressure at the Equator. Once the wind funnels through the isthmus, it fans out to the southwest on the western shore of the gulf, between Puerto Angel and Salina Cruz, and to the southeast on the eastern shore, between Salina Cruz and Puerto Madero.

During the worst season, October through April (the peak is in January), the winds can blow in excess of Force 8 on the Beaufort scale. The commercial port of Salina Cruz, sitting at the head of the gulf, experiences 140 days per year with Force 8 winds. Though Tehuantepec winds are less fierce from May to September, the risk of hurricanes is present.

PREDICTION

The Tehuantepecker is nearly impossible to predict by local cloud observation and onboard barometer readings. It strikes suddenly and lasts anywhere from a few hours to several days. The Pacific weather stations of NMC, KMI and WWV broadcast existing gales in the area, not predicted gales, so they are not sufficient by themselves. You must anticipate weather conditions by becoming your own onboard meteorologist, and then make your own predictions in order not to get caught.

Because the weather conditions that generate gales in the Tehuantepec begin in the Gulf of Mexico, the wise boater will listen to the weather reports from NMN (voice) and NMG (fax) which are broadcast from the US East Coast. See the chapter on MexWX broadcasting for times and frequencies.

What do you listen for? A cold front moving into the Gulf of Mexico from northwest. In advance of the front, the prevailing easterly wind will shift to the southeast and south in the Gulf of Mexico. As the cold front passes, high pressure builds behind it. When this high moves in over Texas, the wind in the Gulf of Mexico clocks around to the north. When the wind is in this quadrant it lines up with the isthmus valley and funnels strongly into the Pacific.

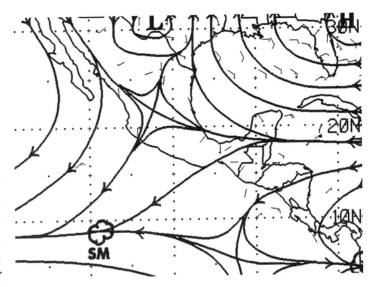

Fig. 13. A low pressure system over Texas creates light south winds across the Isthmus of Tehuantepec and a window to scoot safely across the Gulf of Tehuantepec.

What conditions predict a safe transit? Listen to the portion of the NMN forecast that pertains to the southwest Gulf of Mexico. In advance of a cold front, if the wind is out of the south, you have a chance to scoot across. This weather window may last only a few hours. (Fig. 13) Occasionally a cold front will stall out in the Gulf of Mexico and then begin moving toward the northeast as a warm front, causing a south wind to last for a longer period. In spite of these south winds in the Gulf of Mexico, you won't see them on the Pacific side. The best you can hope for is that the north wind will diminish. Go for it!

TACTICS

TRANSIT THE GULF OF TEHUANTEPEC BY HUGGING THE COAST BETWEEN HUATULCO AND PUERTO MADERO.

Inexperienced skippers resist this "one-foot-on-the-beach" tactic for two reasons.

First, this seems like going out of the way, but veterans who have been hammered in the Tehuantepec know it's the only way. Cutting in shore adds only 30 miles to the total straight-line distance between Puerto Angel and Puerto Madero. Because the Tehuantepecker is an offshore wind, being in close to shore puts your boat in the very narrow lee of the beach berm where the seas remain relatively flat.

Second, general rules say that if you don't know the waters, allow yourself plenty of sea room. However, the eastern side of the Gulf of Tehuantepec is the exception to that rule, and following that rule is very dangerous, even for commercial vessels, let alone pleasure boats.

If you go off shore, the wind begins instantly, rises quickly, and has unlimited room to build seas, has unabated fetch; the seas build to dangerous heights in minutes. The strongest gales can reach out 500 miles from the beach, so trying to outflank them is going WAY out of your way. Almost every season, some inexperienced boaters try making an "end run" on the Gulf of Tehuantepec but end up having to be rescued, often losing their boats, sometimes losing their lives.

The safer tactic is to know how to predict a Tehuantepecker and know the little tricks of navigating the shoreline. I've sailed and powered this gulf in 50-knot winds with sand blowing off the beach onto the deck, with only a little spray or movement in the flat water. However, the safe tactic requires that you have HF radio, good radar and good depth sounder, and are proficient at using them all to steer clear of trouble.

Southbound approaches to Tehuantepec:

Southbound out of Acapulco, if a Tehuantepecker is blowing, you can enter Puerto Angel or Huatulco, the last two sheltered anchorages on the western side of the Gulf of Tehuantepec.

Transiting in this direction is more difficult than coming up from Costa Rica or the Panama Canal, because when you're heading northeast toward Salina Cruz, you can't hug the first part of the shoreline due to rocks and irregularities. However, you can stay about one mile off. Radar is very important; so is your depth sounder. The wind will remain on your bow until you pass Salina Cruz, where it will come onto your beam and then slowly shift aft. Resist the temptation to put into Salina Cruz, because the wind howls endlessly. However, if you must, there's a small-boat anchorage off the beach immediately east of the harbor entrance.

Bahia Ventuosa (Windy Bay) is the very heart of the gulf, where the wind will be the strongest, and it will be on your beam. Fortunately, Ventuosa is a rather narrow inlet adjacent to Salina Cruz, on its east side. Once you make it to the beach east of Bahia Ventuosa you have it made, because the wind will begin to shift aft of your beam and — from here on out — the beach and bottom near shore remain mostly regular and are quite navigable close in. You can run safely in five fathoms of water only a couple of hundred yards off the beach. Again, radar and depth sounder are always being monitored as you gradually curve your course. If the wind becomes overpowering, put down your storm anchor close to shore and ride it out.

The only breaks in this gradually curving shoreline are two lagoon entrances that present shoals just offshore:

➜ Boca de San Francisco into Laguna Inferior, GPS position 15°58.23'North by 93°57.28'West.

➜ Boca de Tonala into Laguna Mar Muerto, GPS position 16°09.63'North by 94°44.96'West.

At both these lagoon entrances, you have to move out to the 10-fathom curve, which is farther off shore than their charted positions. The wind increases in strength near them, because it swoops out from the lagoons. Also, you'll be going slightly farther off shore, so you'll get a taste of what it would have felt like if you had gone straight across. Once you're around Puerto Arista the wind should begin to taper off.

Transiting Tehuantepec toward Costa Rica can be more difficult for sailboats because they may not have the power to motor straight into the wind along the western shore in order to get up into the lee of the beach just east of Salina Cruz. One of my crossings illustrates this situation:

We turned the corner into the Gulf of Tehuantepec on New Year's Day in a 39-foot sailboat heading toward Panama. We actually had a tail-wind and a following current and were making excellent speed wing and wing. I rejoiced at my good fortune. We had made it a good ways into the gulf and were approaching the headland of Morro Ayutla, only 38 miles to Salina Cruz. Ahead I saw white water. As we drew abreast of the point, our tail-wind suddenly dropped, turned completely around on the nose, and began blowing 25 knots. The steep seas were close together and kept getting their tops blown off. Motoring against them proved impossible.

I decided to high-tail it back to Huatulco, 22 miles west, and there to wait it out. With this new wind it should have been an easy downwind retreat, but as we pulled away from Morro Ayutla, the wind dropped and hauled around again — onto our nose. So now I had to motor against the very wind and current that had carried me this far. My conclusion: this place just sucks.

While anchored in Huatulco for five days, we stayed glued to the radio for weather reports. (These were my early days of yacht delivery, before I figured out how to interpolate reports from the Gulf of Mexico, as explained above.) When NMC San Francisco finally dropped their gale warnings for Tehuantepec, we departed pronto.

Motoring in light winds past Morro Ayutla, we got into 20-knot head winds, but the sea wasn't as bad as before. Progressing slowly, I still didn't have enough power to stay as close to the shore as I wanted, so I had to slant off on a port tack to get enough drive from the main to make any headway at all.

At dawn I was abeam of Salina Cruz and five miles off shore. Suddenly we were overwhelmed by a huge wall of wind that gusted to 60 knots. We quickly triple reefed the main, rolled out a tiny portion of the roller furling jib and ran off on the port tack with wind slightly aft. Fortunately I was far enough into the gulf that I could hold a southeasterly course; this allowed us to eventually close with the beach as it gradually angled more southward on the eastern side of Tehuantepec.

But it was hairy for an hour. With my safety harness hooked to the helm, I got sloshed around the cockpit several times by waves pounding over the transom. But by noon it was flat calm.

As we go to press, this above example is the only time in 50 trips in which I've ever had delays in crossing the Tehuantepec. That's because I'm more often delivering power boats and coming up from Panama and Costa Rica, which is the easier direction.

Northbound approaches to Tehuantepec:

Transiting Tehuantepec from Puerto Madero toward Acapulco is easier, because you can stay in the lee of the regular beach during the first part — the eastern side — and then you're running off along the irregular rocky second part — the western side.

From Puerto Madero, run close to the gradually curving shoreline in about five fathoms. A big swell noticed upon leaving Puerto Madero indicates gale winds farther up the line. If a big storm is brewing, the winds may begin to blow at about Solo Dios. Sand may blow on deck, but as long as you stay in the lee of the beach, seas will not have enough fetch to build. However, be ready to turn out briefly and quickly return to the shoreline in order to get around these two lagoon entrances:

→Boca de Tonala into Laguna Mar Muerto, GPS position 16°09.63'North by 94°44.96'West.

→Boca de San Francisco into Laguna Inferior, GPS position 15°58.23'North by 93°57.28'West.

Once you reach Salina Cruz, turn to the southwest and put the wind aft. Still stay about a mile off shore until the wind and following seas begin to diminish, usually at about Morro Ayutla except in the strongest of gales.

SUMMER and FALL

The water mass just offshore of the Gulf of Tehuantepec is the principal area of hurricane genesis. The first storm of the year forms here usually during the last week of May. Hurricane season ends more gradually than it begins, usually by November first.

If you have to transit this gulf between May and October, do so with extreme caution, have good radar and a fast and powerful boat, staying close to shore; cyclonic storms form off shore and stay off shore. (Sailboats shouldn't be anywhere near this area in summer.) In a 25-year study done by the Mexican Meteorological Service, only three storms actually touched the shore of the Gulf of Tehuantepec. But in the 1997 El Niño season, two hurricanes landed in Tehuantepec.

WINTER and SPRING

The weather patterns in the southern US and Gulf of Mexico that open and close the window across the Gulf of Tehuantepec occur from the end of hurricane season through winter and into May. Late November, all through December and January, and into February you can expect cold fronts to push down into lower Texas and the southwest Gulf of Mexico. In advance of these cold fronts, look for gales to decrease in the Gulf of Tehuantepec and be ready to scoot across. When the cold front moves across and high pressure fills in behind it, your window will come slamming closed, so you'd better not still be there.

Also, Trade Winds are at their highest throughout the winter months.

BEST TIMES TO TRANSIT TEHUANTEPEC?

The two best times to transit the Gulf of Tehuantepec safely are the first of November and the first of May, which are at the end of one hurricane season and just before the beginning of the next.

Gulf of Tehuantepec

Chapter 7

Focus: Central America's Gulf of Papagallo

⁓⁓⁓⁓⁓⁓⁓⁓⁓⁓⁓⁓⁓⁓⁓⁓⁓

If you enter Mexico from the south or depart south to cruise Costa Rica, then you need to know about weather in Guatemala, Nicaragua and the Gulf of Papagallo.

Geographically, this small gulf lies between Cabo Velas and Cabo Santa Elena, both of which lie in northern Costa Rica. But the region of ocean affected by winds in the Gulf of Papagallo extends from Costa Rica's Cabo Velas to Punta Remedios in El Salvador. That includes approximately 32,400 square miles of sea surface and the coastlines of Nicaragua, Honduras and El Salvador. (Fig. 14) "Papagallo" (pah-pah-GUY-oh) is one of several Spanish words for "parrot," and wild parrots are still common along much of this 425-mile-long coastline. Perhaps the Spanish explorers found parrots being blown out to sea during these wind storms.

Gales in the Gulf of Papagallo are just as notorious as those of Tehuantepec, but Papagallo has its own unique set of formation conditions, dangers and tactics for minimizing trouble.

WINTER and SPRING

During the winter months (January is the worst), cold fronts reaching down into the Caribbean augment the force of the northeast Trade Winds, and these winds bridge the backbone of Central America at its lowest spot and blow strongly into the Pacific.

The low spot is the Rio San Juan Valley on the Nicaragua-Costa Rica border. Winds are strongest and easterly at the head of the Gulf of Papagallo. Depending upon where in the larger region you encounter Papagallo winds, their direction may be anywhere from north through southeast. Unfortunately, no weather warnings are broadcast over commercial high-seas stations for this region, even though winds occasionally reach gale force and blow for several days.

Gulf of Papagallo

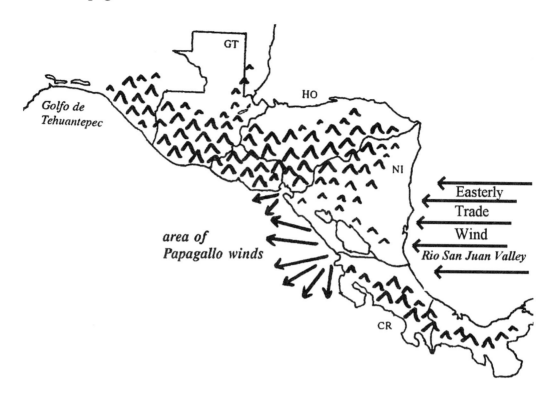

Fig. 14. Strong headwinds often come as an unpleasant surprise to many southbound boaters in the Gulf of Papagallo.

SUMMER and FALL

Hurricane Season: Pacific hurricanes begin as tropical disturbances as early as the end of May. Mexico's Gulf of Tehuantepec is their primary formation zone, though they occasionally form farther south, including the waters off Guatemala and El Salvador.

Costa Rica itself is south of the hurricane belt and consequently is a favorite summering-over spot for long-range cruisers. Summer brings thunderstorms with lightning and occasional waterspouts to Costa Rica, though these intense rain storms are never of long duration or contain sustained winds of hurricane strength.

To be truly safe, vessels that have summered over in Costa Rica shouldn't leave to return north until November 1.

However, fast powerboats with long cruising range can, and do, make this leg during the summer months. The trick is to travel in the proper slot between easterly waves. Since these waves move from east to west, a vessel traveling from Costa Rica northwest to Mexico has the best chance of staying between waves.

Traveling in the opposite direction is much more difficult, because you will be closing with these waves at a rapid rate, so you'll have very little time/space between them. If you're southbound from Mexico, you should be in northern Costa Rica before the last week in May. Read the section on easterly waves in the Hurricane Season chapter.

RADIO INFORMATION

Monitor voice weather from NMN or fax station NMG for weather in the Caribbean, and see the chapter on MexWX Broadcasts for times and frequencies. If a cold front is passing and the Trade Winds are blowing northeast 20 knots or above in the southwest Caribbean, then the likelihood of strong wind in the Papagallo is high.

Also listen to the Central American Breakfast Club, a ham radio network at 1300 Zulu on 7.085 MHz lower sideband. Though this net does not give specific weather reports, a shore station in Playas del Coco (10°34' North by 85°43' West) frequently relates the weather at that location, which is inside Costa Rica's Gulf of Papagallo. If the wind is blowing heavy in Playas del Coco, it will be blowing in the entire Papagallo region.

ROUTING ACROSS PAPAGALLO

The route you should take depends upon which direction you're traveling and what time of year it is:

Southbound: This is usually the more difficult direction of travel because you'll be heading straight into the wind and seas. Although, if the wind has any east to it, you can get a lee by staying in close to shore.

At any time of year, head to a waypoint off Guatemala (14°04' North by 91°52' West). This passes outside the 10-fathom curve off Champerico and San Jose. Do not pass closer than this because of shoaling southeast of Champerico and much shrimp-boat traffic. I've been boarded by the Guatemalan Navy as much as 30 miles offshore. They are courteous but dead serious. They've inspected us and let us proceed.

From Guatemala, head to 13°09' North, 88°54' West, which is offshore of the Rio Lempa, El Salvador. Then lay a course to 12°52'North, 87°45' West (five miles off shore of Punta Consiguina), being careful of the Rio Lempa Shoals on this leg. Afterward turn southeast and parallel the coast of Nicaragua five miles offshore.

Gulf of Papagallo

If the weather is rough, head closer in shore. You can seek shelter in the anchorages in the Gulf of Fonseca, Corinto or San Juan del Sur. In late spring, if the weather forecast looks good you could run 10 miles off shore and, if it starts to get rough, head closer in shore.

Northbound: This is the easier direction of travel, because the wind and current are in your favor.

From April 1 through December 15, proceed directly across the Gulf of Papagallo. From five miles abeam Point Guiones (9°49' North by 85°44' West), which is the southwest tip of Costa Rica, head for a waypoint off Guatemala (14°04' North by 91°52' West). Or if you're departing from the Playas del Coco area proceed directly to the waypoint off Guatemala. This is a 440-mile open-ocean crossing with a significant current that generally sets you toward the beach. From this point, proceed directly to Puerto Madero (14°42' North by 92°27' West), the first port in southern Mexico.

If you are northbound in a well-found sailboat, you should have a fast sail because the wind and current are generally in your favor. In a powerboat, the ride is usually a little rough and rolly. If the weather report looks threatening or you have any doubts about whether your sailboat is well-found or if you don't want rock'n roll in your powerboat, then take the following winter route:

From December 16 through March 31, you'll need to take a route closer to shore. At the above waypoint five miles offshore of Pt. Guiones, turn north into the Gulf of Papagallo and stay close to the coast to avoid gale-force winds. You can stay in the area of Marina Flamingo and Playas del Coco until the wind drops somewhat. Then run the reverse of the above southbound route, five miles offshore.

Classic Papagallo: Northwest bound. Here's a classic example of a winter crossing of the Gulf of Papagallo.

My wife, Pat, and I had just departed Puntarenas, Costa Rica, heading to Marina Flamingo in the Papagallo area of northwest Costa Rica to top off our tanks before the long run to Acapulco. Just then, the owner of a local fishing fleet warned us that his boats were reporting a "strong blow" going on in the Gulf of Papagallo. I knew we'd be hugging the coast all the way to Flamingo.

As we cleared the sand spit at Puntarenas, even the Gulf of Nicoya was unusually windy. Staying close in around the Nicoya Peninsula, our wind subsided, and we motored along under a full moon on glassy seas until we rounded Pt. Guiones and turned northward toward the Papagallo. The wind strengthened the farther north we went, but because it was blowing offshore, we had no serious seas this close in. We entered Bahia Potrero and came to anchor just before dawn.

The wind was higher than normal and gusty inside Potrero Bay, but the bottom provides good holding. We decided to stay at anchor for a day or two, hoping to see an expected wind drop before we tackled the infamous Gulf of Papagallo. I decided that when we departed, we'd hug the coast in northern Costa Rica and all along Nicaragua, rather than take a straight shot across the wind-ravaged Papagallo.

The following morning the wind wasn't quite as strong, and the clouds weren't quite as compressed over the hilltops, so I decided to give it a go. As we headed into the very head of the Gulf of Papagallo the wind steadily increased to 40 knots. I wondered if the average cruising sailboat would have had enough power to motor into the wind as we were doing. The ocean surface was crammed with white caps and blowing streaks of foam. Nonetheless the sea around us was flat and we continued to make good progress.

Once we passed the head of the gulf, the wind shifted aft the beam. We cut inside the Islas Murcielagos (Bat Islands) close inshore to Cabo Santa Elena. This is a prime cruising area with many isolated, protected coves. At Cabo Santa Elena we turned directly toward the Nicaragua border. The wind lessened and shifted even more aft. We paralleled Nicaragua's coast about five miles off. Had the wind been stronger I would have moved in closer.

The following morning we neared the entrance to the Golfo de Fonseca which contains the borders of Nicaragua, Honduras and El Salvador. Again, because of the funneling effect, this area develops notorious offshore winds. At this time, the civil war was still raging in El Salvador, so I had no intention of using the same tactic as in the Gulf of Tehuantepec. Instead, I laid a course to cross 10 miles offshore. A ham radio operator in Playas del Coco said he'd just spoken with the American Consulate and that a fresh travel advisory to avoid this area had just been posted.

Fortunately the heavy northeasterly wind had blown itself out, and we safely put Fonseca behind us. The waters off Guatemala were calm as usual, in the lee of huge volcano peaks. That night we witnessed lava pouring out of Volcan Fuego, one of Guatemala's most active cones.

Classic Papagallo: Southeast bound. During the winter months, going toward Costa Rica from Mexico is usually the rougher direction, because you're going against the prevailing wind.

It was February. This time, Pat and I were delivering a luxuriously appointed 57-foot motoryacht from San Diego to Ft. Lauderdale. Political problems in Central America kept us from going inshore. The fax picture from San Francisco showed no wind arrows near the Gulf of Papagallo, and the fax from NAM in Portsmouth showed 15 knots easterly in the western Caribbean. Once we got out there, the weather off the coast of Guatemala was as calm as usual.

But at 18 hours out of Puerto Madero, we started to get a tell-tale swell coming from the southeast, right on the nose. I thought maybe we were in for it — we were. By 24 hours out, conditions were noted in the log book in scrawly hand as "heavy." The worst of it, 30-knot winds kicking up breath-taking 15-foot seas, lasted for the next 36 hours.

We'd been in worse weather and sea conditions, but mostly in well-founded world-cruising sailboats; this was very rough going for a delicate motoryacht. Also, the seas were confused because the wind was shifting 90° from southeast to northeast.

During daylight hours at least we could hand steer around the biggest waves, but at night we couldn't see them coming until their giant white combers were almost waltzing right into our bow, so we had to keep pulling back the throttles for each biggie, then rev back up to speed (as much speed as was tolerable) to avoid getting swamped by the next one. Pat's knuckles were white from gripping the helm and throttles. She said it was like trying to climb an oncoming avalanche without then falling off the back side of it. Almost as soon as the boat recovered from one huge crested wave, wham, another pasted us. Then another. So it went, on and on for many watches.

Eventually, our speed was down to four knots. You can't move much slower than that on a powerboat without losing your steerage way. And we definitely did NOT want to lay in any of those troughs. We were well off shore, and even if we'd been welcome in the few Nicaraguan ports, they were too far to weather. We couldn't lay-to like we would have in a sailboat, and we couldn't run off with it, or we'd run out of fuel about 600 miles from land. There wasn't much we could do except "keep on keeping on" and pray it didn't get worse. Fortunately it just stayed the same.

After 36 hours of very rough going, we arrived exhausted at Playas del Coco, Costa Rica. Once we un-balled the chain and had the hook down safely, we looked in the mirror and saw gray hairs that hadn't been there before that crossing of the Papagallo.

Chapter 8

Hurricanes

Hurricanes are one of nature's most destructive phenomena. Mexico's Pacific coast is subject to these tropical cyclones from late May through the beginning of November. Carib Indians invented the word "hurricane" which comes from the name of their god of the winds. Caribbean hurricanes are different from those formed on the Pacific coast of Mexico, but there's a similarity in how they're generated.

LIFE CYCLE OF A TROPICAL HURRICANE

Hurricane season on the west side of Mexico begins with the northward movement into Mexican waters of the Intertropical Convergence Zone (ITCZ). Generally located around the earth's equatorial region, the ITCZ is generated when intense overhead sun heats up the sea's surface, warming and moistening the air above it. This moist unstable air begins to rise – and then condenses as it cools and falls as rain. Thus, the ITCZ is an area of strong ascending air currents, a great deal of cloudiness and frequent heavy showers and thunderstorms.

The ITCZ moves in response to the sun's movement – north and south of the Equator – due to the inclination of the earth's axis to its orbit about the sun. Because the sun is overhead in the northern hemisphere during the mid-year months, it causes the ITCZ to migrate to Mexican waters. A two-month lag time separates the sun's actual maximum declination from the position of the ITCZ.

While the ITCZ remains near the Equator, only small and weak disturbances can develop. But as it migrates away from the Equator and toward the Mexican coast, the revolution of the earth on its axis can create sufficient counter-clockwise spin on rising air currents to encourage the formation of tropical storms and hurricanes. The counter-clockwise spin is the Coriolis effect. Its direction is reversed on the other side of the Equator.

Hurricanes derive their tremendous energy and thus their violence from the latent heat of condensation (598 calories per gram). That heat is released into the atmosphere as water vapor condenses from the heating of the sea surface by the overhead sun. As long as the hurricane center remains over warm water, its energy supply is almost limitless.

Hurricanes

Here's what has to be present in order for a hurricane to develop:
1. An extant tropical depression at the surface.
2. The depression travels across the surface at less than 13 knots.
3. Barometric pressure below 1004 millibars in the low latitudes and higher than normal in the high latitudes.
4. Sea-surface temperature of 78.8° F or higher.
5. Vigorous rain or rain showers in the vicinity.
6. Winds from the east extending up to at least 30,000 feet but diminishing with height.
7. The upper air flow near 40,000 feet has special dynamic conditions.

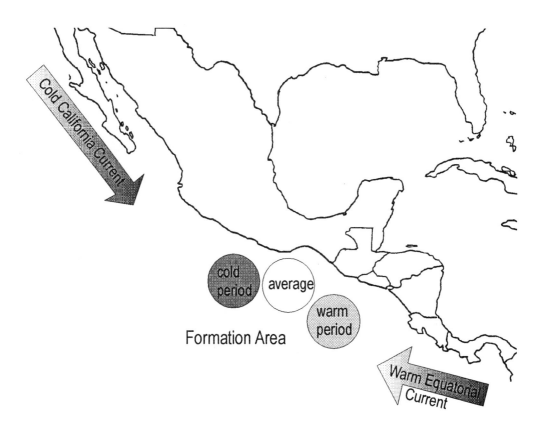

Fig. 15. The hurricane genesis area moves throughout the season, depending on displacement by cold or warm currents.

Mexican hurricanes develop in the Gulf of Tehuantepec at about latitude 15° north. This hurricane-genesis region varies with the position of maximum maritime heating, which is subject to the interactive movements of the Cold California Current and the Warm Counter-Equatorial Currents. Consequently tropical disturbances can sometimes form as much as 300 miles southwest of this region. (Fig. 15) A tropical disturbance can be a tropical depression, a tropical storm, or a full-blown tropical hurricane.

A few of the early-season tropical disturbances lack power, recurve soon and hit the coast near Acapulco, but most continue offshore in a west-northwest direction where they die en route toward Hawaii. (Fig. 16) As the season progresses each

Fig. 16. June hurricanes have short runs close to the mainland and a tendency to slam ashore farther south.

Fig. 17. July hurricanes have longer runs and may strike Baja California.

storm or hurricane gathers more power and travels farther north, and those alive during August and September may punch land.

August is the most active month; an average formation of 4.3 tropical disturbances form then, and 2.2 of these reach hurricane strength. (Fig. 18) In this period they have their greatest forward speeds — an average of 7 to 12 knots with an upper

Fig. 18. August hurricnaes can reach farther north and west.

Fig. 19. September hurricanes have a marked tendency to slam into Baja California.

Hurricanes

Fig. 20. October storms tend to recurve and hit the coast.

limit of an astonishing 25 knots. That's forward motion; how many vessels could outrun such a storm?

By October the statistical incidence rate has dropped, but these late-season storms are particularly dangerous. They become very erratic, are able to intensify rapidly, and frequently recurve and hit the Mexican coast. (Fig. 20)

Normally hurricanes do not travel beyond 30°north latitude, because the California Cold Current is a storm destroyer. If a tropical cyclone passes over the cold current, it is denied the warm sea surface necessary for unstable tropical air currents, so its supply of water vapor diminishes, and thus its source of energy is cut off. The 30°N-limit has exceptions, and on very rare occasions weakened storms will touch Southern California and Arizona.

DEMISE OF HURRICANE SEASON

The first 15 days of October historically mark the final blast of hurricane season, but during years or periods of high cyclonic activity, tropical storms and hurricanes have occurred in November. They are usually weak and have short runs, because the advancing autumn season tends to cool off oceanic waters in the formation area. The sun's rays are no longer overhead and the Cold California Current penetrates farther south.

The primary reason for the end of hurricane season is directly related to beginning of the season of Northers in the Gulf of Tehuantepec. (See Fig. 11) The north winds push surface waters out in the direction of their axes. As water moves in to replace this water, it generates two currents, one toward the southeast, parallel to the coast of the state of Oaxaca, and the other toward the northwest parallel to the coast of the state of Chiapas. These currents are fed by profoundly cold waters. The mixing of this cold and warm water reduces sea surface temperatures to only one or two degrees above the air temperature in this region, creating a temperature inversion. This generates a completely stable atmospheric equilibrium, essentially a lid to prevent air and moisture from rising. Thus tropical depressions can no longer form. The introduction of cold waters in the Gulf of Tehuantepec was proven by infra-red photos taken by weather satellites NOAA 2 and 3 in an investigation related to tuna fishing made by the French Meteorological Service and supported by information from ships in the area.

HURRICANE PREDICTION

Operating in Mexican waters in the summer months is very dangerous and is best left to experienced professionals. Even for those captains, operating small craft after July 15 is hazardous. Except within certain summering-over areas, sail boats are at great risk. Fast powerboats with good range, operated by knowledgeable captains, can and do run the Mexican coast in hurricane season, outrunning bad weather. However they must constantly make themselves aware of current weather conditions throughout the region and, further, be able to recognize conditions that may lead to hurricane formation. If they wait too long and sea conditions turn rough, they can no longer run fast and may be overtaken by the full fury of a hurricane.

For years I had turned down deliveries that involved going through the Panama Canal after July. Even though I'd studied tropical weather patterns for more than a decade, I didn't feel I could get enough timely data to predict when conditions were ripe for hurricane formation in the Pacific.

Weather faxes from NMC in San Francisco showed only tropical disturbances AFTER they had formed. As a result, I'd often found myself traveling on the fringe of a tropical depression 24 hours or more before it showed up on the fax! This was due to a lack of data gathering and also to a delay in reporting. And there simply was no chart from NMC to help me anticipate conditions that lead to Pacific hurricane development.

I never thought to look at charts for the East Coast to get data that would allow me to predict tropical weather disturbances in the Pacific.

Then I discovered the 36-hour Prognosis Blend from NAM, the Navy fax station formerly located in Portsmouth, Virginia. This chart covers the North Atlantic and Caribbean but also covers a small portion of the Eastern Pacific as far west as Acapulco. I knew previously that traveling in the Caribbean in the summer meant you had to watch for "easterly waves" on this chart. In combination with satellite photos I would have a good idea of each waves' present location plus speed and direction of travel. NMG now has charts showing easterly waves.

An easterly wave (see Definitions below) is a northward bulge in isobar lines, and it travels from east to west in the Trade Wind belt. Ahead of these waves the weather is partly cloudy and wind comes from the northeast. As the wave passes over your position, the cloud cover increases, rain comes more frequently in squalls, and the wind shifts to the southeast. This gradual transition zone is 30 to 100 miles in width. If upper atmospheric conditions are just right, an easterly wave can develop a closed circulation of its own capable of reaching hurricane strength.

That was all well and good for the Caribbean, but then I discovered that these waves often cross from the Caribbean into the Pacific. They are only found on the aforementioned chart from the East Coast. I was excited when I first made this discovery while sitting in my own weather fax-equipped office in San Diego. I saw an

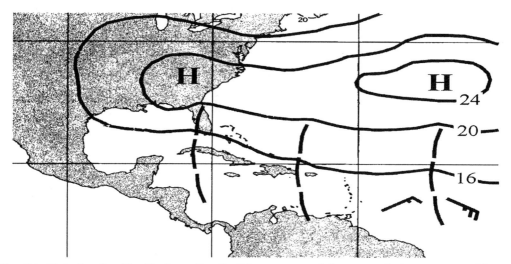

Fig. 21. Entering the Pacific from the Caribbean, any of these easterly waves could form a hurricane in the Gulf of Tehuantepec.

easterly wave about to pass from Central American waters into the Gulf of Tehuantepec (Fig. 21), so I predicted that a tropical depression would form within 24 hours. Sure enough, a day later the depression showed on the San Francisco chart.

WAVE-RIDING TACTICS

How does one get through this dangerous area? The tactic is to travel between easterly waves and stay in a safe port while one is passing near your location.

Only a small percentage of easterly waves ever become depressions, but each one must be watched carefully. They occur approximately every 15 degrees of longitude, which gives you about 900 miles between them. A period of as short as three to four days separates their passage, so the tricky tactic is to travel in the slot half way in between them, in the safe-weather window of opportunity. Since easterly waves travel at speeds of 10 to 13 knots, you can see why only fast power boats should attempt traveling in this season.

Figure 22 is an easterly wave timeline. The ideal time to depart on this trip leg would be 12 hours after the passage of the trough.

Much of Mexico's southern coastline runs on an east-west axis. That means vessels bound from southern to northern Mexico are traveling in the favored direction. Vessels traveling in the opposite direction, however, are closing with these waves at a faster rate, so the windows of opportune are much smaller. In fact, impossibly small. Cruisers should use the above information wisely and not take chances. The prudent thing to do is find a safe place to hole up for the hurricane season. As a yacht delivery captain, I'm paid to handle large, fast, well-equipped, long-range vessels

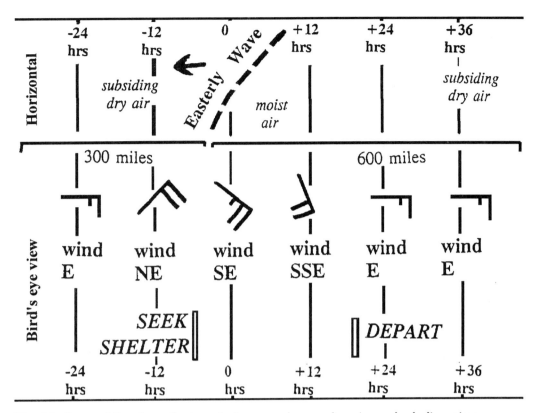

Fig. 22. General timeline of an easterly wave: know when to seek shelter, stay anchored and to depart.

staffed with experienced professionals; I wouldn't attempt this region in hurricane season in anything less than:

→ A good strong sea boat with reliable engine.

→ At least a 10-knot capability with at least 1000-mile range.

→ Heavy ground tackle.

→ The ability to continually monitor weather reports and plot all positions of easterly waves and tropical disturbances.

Some rules to remember:

→ Always know where the nearest safe shelter is.

→ If you're in a safe port and a storm is forming, stay put.

→ If you're at sea, scoot to a safe port ASAP.

→ Don't go way offshore, because this is where storms form; being in shore gives more time to make port.

→ In spite of all the theories, satellite pictures and weather fax charts, that phenomenon called Luck is still a factor.

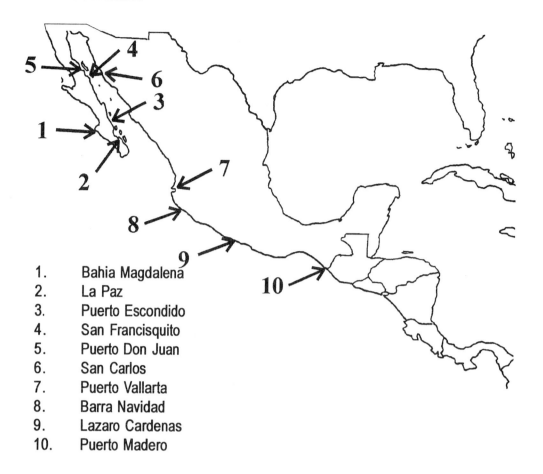

1. Bahia Magdalena
2. La Paz
3. Puerto Escondido
4. San Francisquito
5. Puerto Don Juan
6. San Carlos
7. Puerto Vallarta
8. Barra Navidad
9. Lazaro Cardenas
10. Puerto Madero

HURRICANE HOLES

No Mexican ports are "safe" in hurricanes, but a few ports listed above enjoy histories of offering varying degrees of protection. These ports are either outside the beaten path of most hurricanes, or nearby mountains deflect most of their power. Notice we said "most" hurricanes.

1. Bahia Magdalena

Mag Bay, as we gringos call it, is a huge watery area more like an inland sea. Inside the barrier islands are several possible hurricane holes, but the bay's very size works to its disadvantage. Although you might find protection from the wind in one semicircle, if the hurricane eye passes over you and the wind shifts, you may then find yourself on a lee shore – now with winds from several miles of fetch coming at you from across the bay. Finding protection from the east is the most difficult because the whole terrain east of Mag Bay is flat and the eastern side of Mag Bay is generally very shallow, making it difficult to get close enough to that shoreline to get protection.

Belcher's Point is Mag Bay's most commonly used anchorage for prevailing weather because it lies two miles northwest of Punta Entrada. But Belcher's is not a hurricane berth; hurricane swell coming in through the entrance to the bay reaches Belcher's, and it's wide open to the east and the large fetch in that direction.

During the 1997 El Nino season, I became intimate with Mag Bay while looking for shelter from Hurricane Nora. She was a very slow moving hurricane that kept us pinned down inside Mag Bay for eight days. Here are my findings:

No Name Cove (24°31.24' North, 111°58.16' West)

Capitan Rodriguez, the Port Captain of Puerto San Carlos, recommended this spot to me. It was here that we rode out Hurricane Nora.

This cove is 2.5 miles east of Punta Redonda and sheltered from winds E to WNW by the 1,700' high mountains that form the barrier island of Isla Margarita. In prevailing northwesterlies this is a lee shore. But as a hurricane berth, the mountains knock down the wind from the primary storm direction and the seas won't reach here from the bay entrance. The water is deep, so you need to get close to shore to find 40' of water. Even that requires that you put out 280' of rode to get storm scope. The bottom is gravelly, so you need to back down and use power to drag your anchor around until you can get it to set firmly.

Here are some notes from our log during Nora:

A few hours after we anchored at No Name yesterday, the first rain squalls come through, and the wind began to puff up from ESE. We stood continuous anchor watch night and day. This morning the wind has increased to 40 knots in the gusts. We barely have a lee, and a 3-foot wind chop is coming at us from the east. This 98-footer has been sheering around at anchor about 180° and we often are laying in the trough. It is irritating and uncomfortable, but not dangerous. The important thing is that the anchor is holding....

Fortunately Nora has now weakened somewhat and is continuing NW, and her center is now due to pass 150 miles offshore of us. This is our second day in our hurricane berth, and I think this will be Nora's CPA (closest point of approach). The wind is still gusting well in excess of 45 knots with sea smoke. Squalls strike the water and swirl mist off the sea surface like dust devils in the desert....

Nora was right abeam of us, and then she began to recurve. (We had some anxious hours earlier when two separate reports showed that Nora was taking a sudden 90 degree turn to the east, straight at us. I doubted this could happen, and in fact it now turns out that it didn't.) However Nora is slowly curving from NW to north and she may remain equidistant from us for about the next 18 hours at her CPA....

Hurricanes

Finally Hurricane Nora is beginning to move away. The wind has clocked around to the south, giving us a better lee from Isla Margarita, and we aren't lying beam on to the swell...

Hurricane Nora has began to pick up her forward speed from 8 knots to 18 knots. The barometer has begun to rise, and the wind has dropped off considerably.

Lucky for us, but not so for Turtle Bay: Nora stomped right on it.

The wind didn't shift to the northwest as I'd feared, therefore No Name gave us protection throughout the storm. If the center of the storm had passed directly over us, with winds shifting northward, we'd have been on a lee shore. If that had happened, I would have cut and run off downwind to Puerto Alcatraz.

Puerto Alcatraz (24°30.6' North, 111°51.1' West)

Puerto Alcatraz anchorage is a small shallow cove 10 miles inside Mag Bay from the entrance and located on the west bank the Canal de Gaviota. The Gaviota Channel is the entrance to Bahia Almejas, the southern part of Mag Bay. The cove consists of a low sandy hook which gives protection from the north and west. The sandy hook's narrow neck is submerged at high tide and it's tip becomes an island. By tucking up in the northeast corner of his tiny bay you can get all-around protection, anchoring in about 12 feet over sand bottom. I looked into this spot before Hurricane Nora struck, but I decided against it because the land was so low to the southeast, and Capt. Rodriguez said it was not a hurricane berth.

However during Nora we had radio contact with the skipper and crew of an engineless sailboat who were riding it out in Alcatraz. Although they had stronger winds from the SE than we did, they reported themselves to be "snug as a bug in a rug." Had the eye of the hurricane passed over us, along with its shifting winds, they would have had better all-around protection.

Laguna de Islotes (24°44.5' North, 112°02.6' West)

Before Hurricane Nora was eminent, I decided to survey an area (12 miles north from the entrance to Mag Bay) called Laguna de los Islotes whose shallow entrance gives access to a possible hurricane hole with all-around protection in the mangroves. At high tide we anchored in 12 feet, 1.3 miles from the lagoon entrance and put our launch in the water. What I discovered is that we were then getting a swell coming in from (Mag Bay's) entrance, 12 miles to the south. On the bar at the lagoon entrance we sounded out a dog-leg course across the bar with a minimum depth of 10.5' which, adjusted for tide, equates to 5' at a chart datum of mean low water. It is lined with mangroves and cordon cactus.

Once inside this lagoon, we rode for miles in at least 20' of water. At first I thought it would be a great hurricane hole. However when I went back across the bar only an hour later, the afternoon wind had picked up, the southerly swell had increased, and the tide was ebbing strongly across the bar; it was quite rough. I *decided against the risk of taking our 5.8' draft vessel with fin stabilizers (worth $5 million) across that bar even on the next high tide, because the swell was bound to increase as Nora approached—which it has. I just didn't want to risk losing her on the bar.*

However, Laguna de Islotes is still worth keeping in mind. If it looks like the eye of a hurricane is going to hit, if you have sufficient time and the right high-slack tide to send the dinghy ahead to sound your way in, and if you're on a boat with a keel to protect your screws if you touch, then it just might be the answer.

2. La Paz

The harbor itself is not a hurricane hole nor, in my opinion, is it a good place to summer over. The harbor is too exposed to a broad fetch from north winds. (I witnessed the damage that a 1976 hurricane did here: All along the "downtown" anchorage, heavy seas from northerly winds gouged away huge stretches of the coast road, eroded the side streets into deep arroyos, and destroyed many buildings on the inland side of the coast road.)

Marina Palmira, just north of town, might survive because they built a surrounding breakwater. You can also haul your boat out there and leave her "on the hard." As safe as that might sound, in the same yard a 1996 hurricane knocked down six sailboats in a row, like dominoes. Under all that stress and windage, the cradles weren't strong enough or anchored well enough to the ground to survive.

Pichilingue, the commercial and ferry harbor about five miles north of La Paz, is the traditional hurricane anchorage, because it offers all-round protection. In fact the Port Captain generally allows no one to anchor there unless a hurricane watch is in effect. As many as 100 boats have anchored in here. As in any crowded hurricane anchorage, a secondary danger is having someone's anchor fouling yours or dragging into you.

3. Puerto Escondido

Boaters summering over in the middle latitudes of the Sea of Cortez use Puerto Escondido, just south of Loreto, as a hurricane refuge. The inner harbor measures about one mile by 1.5 miles and is almost land-locked. Theoretically, the surrounding low hills and land bridges provide some shelter in all directions from tropical disturbances traveling up the Sea of Cortez. The sheer eastern face of Las Gigantas mountains rises west of the port, so storms crossing the Baja California peninsula from the Pacific are forced aloft, and their full force isn't felt in the port. Two precautions here are flash-flood inundations coming down from those mountains, and tangled anchors due to over-crowding in this popular port.

Hurricanes

4. Caleta San Francisquito (28°25.7' North, 112°52.9' West)

Often cruisers summering over in the Sea of Cortez move as far north as Bahia Los Angles to get farther away from the main hurricane belt. However even this far north, hurricanes tend to cross over the Baja peninsula from the Pacific, usually headed NE in their recurvature phase. Caleta San Francisquito, located 43 miles south of LA Bay, is a tiny pocket bay with a narrow entrance which should give good protection. However draft is a consideration. The entrance has 4' of water at minus tides and 6' in the middle. However if you draw less than 6' you should be able to enter at high tide. I've seen 8' draft shrimpers inside. Favor the northeast corner.

5. Puerto Don Juan (28°58.0'North, 113°27.5' West)

A land-locked pocket bay on the eastern approaches to LA Bay, Don Juan has a narrow entrance with plenty of water and opens up into an area larger than Caleta San Francisquito. There is even a small interior bay called the Bath Tub, and a careening beach. Don Juan's eastern end shoals, and you should always watch the tide range (11.5 feet). Flies are reported to be a problem in the summer, but a hurricane breeze should dispel them.

LA Bay is generally a great region in which to summer over. You can cruise the many anchorages in the islands, keeping alert to the weather. When a hurricane threatens, scoot to Puerto Don Juan and button up. Quite a number of boats could anchor here in 25 feet of water in a storm.

6. San Carlos (27°56.1' North, 111°03.5'West)

Operating in the northern half of the Sea of Cortez is possible in the summer, because if you are paying close attention to the weather reports, you should have time to seek shelter. San Carlos, near Guaymas on the mainland, is also a land-locked port surrounded by mountains, but its mountains shelter it primarily from the east.

San Carlos was ravaged by Hurricane Lester in 1992. Most of the boat damage occurred in the outer anchorage, caused by unattended vessels dragging others onto the surf-pounded beach. Marina San Carlos is building new breakwaters in the outer anchorage. You can haul out your boat in San Carlos and leave it safely "on the hard" for the season.

Mazatlan regularly gets hit by hurricanes, so don't plan to be here during summer. However, in an emergency, the new man-made basin of Marina Mazatlan, located six miles north of Mazatlan's old commercial harbor, might prove to be a worthy hurricane hole for small boats. The stubby jetty-lined entrance channel contains a baffle, and then a narrower channel leads eastward into the more land-locked basin. The channel will become closed out by breakers as storms approach, so get in early. Shrimpers and small freighters head deep into the mangroves that extend inland and south from the town's old harbor.

7. Puerto Vallarta (20°39' North, 105°15' West)

Puerto Vallarta's two marinas are the safest hurricane hideouts on the whole coast. The mountain range that runs west-southwest toward Cabo Corrientes on the south side of Banderas Bay is an effective barrier to hurricanes. What remnants that do enter Banderas Bay can savage boats anchored out in the open roadsteads, so get into Marina Vallarta or the older Marina Vallarta Norte.

On the first of October, 1996 we were ready to depart La Paz to the south, but a tropical depression had just formed south of Acapulco. However I determined that at 10 knots we should be able to safely beat it into Puerto Vallarta, 400 miles southeast. I also had the options of diverting to Mazatlan or San Blas, so I departed early that morning.

By late afternoon of the first day out, the tropical depression had already become Tropical Storm Hernan, and it was expected to become a hurricane in 48 hours. Our winds stayed light northerly, although we began to feel a long-period swell coming out of the south. As we closed with the mainland, clouds and lightning began to appear in the southern sky. After a 40-hour run we safely made it into Marina Vallarta.

The morning after our arrival, weather reports said that the eye of full-blown Hurricane Hernan was just off shore, raking the Mexican coastline from Manzanillo north, and she was headed our way. We took down the bimini top, doubled up our lines, and put out the big fenders. By the next morning we would know whether PV really is a safe hurricane hole - or not.

Hernan roared ashore near Manzanillo with 70-knot winds and gusts to 85. As she moved north toward PV, the east-west running mountain range south of PV ripped the storm apart. The center of what was left of Hernan passed only a few miles east of us, however we had only a 20-knot gust from a heavy rain squall that lasted about half an hour. The rest of the time the wind was calm, but it rained heavily. PV had proven to be the natural hurricane hole I'd always heard it to be.

South of Puerto Vallarta the coast is very dangerous during summer. Don't even think of summering over there. However, if you are unlucky enough to get caught down south with a storm approaching, here are some ideas:

8. Barra Navidad (19°12.0' North, 104°41.4' West)

Barra Navidad has a dredged lagoon that offers excellent protection behind Punta Graham, provided that you draw six feet or less.

One August, I was delivering a 58' Hatteras LRC from Florida to California at the height of hurricane season. We were pinned down for a week in Acapulco while three hurricanes passed offshore. I finally had a break in storms and jumped

Hurricanes

in behind the third storm after it passed to the northwest of us. Twelve hours after we left, a fourth storm formed behind us. As if that wasn't bad enough, it seemed to be interacting with the one ahead of us – which had become stationary – while the one behind us was picking up speed. It looked like we were about to become dog meat in a giant hurricane sandwich.

I entered Barra Navidad and anchored in the inner basin (where a new marina has since been built, Bahia Grande). We anchored on a sand bottom in about 20' of water and were completely surrounded by land. Southeast of us was a huge mountain, the back side of Punta Graham. From this position, that large land mass would help block the blasts from the primary wind direction for Mexican hurricanes coming up the coast.

The hurricane was downgraded to a tropical storm when it roared into Manzanillo (20 miles away) with 50-knot sustained winds. We never had an anxious moment. The wind never exceeded 20 knots and was for the most part calm. But it rained and rained and rained. The second storm dissipated in Mexico's mountainous interior. Then the storm ahead of us began to move up into the Sea of Cortez and after a 48 hour stay we were able to get back underway.

Manzanillo is a favorite target of hurricanes, but north of the town Laguna San Pedrito has been dredged to form the newer inner harbor. Survival might be possible by running a boat up into the mud and mangroves at the lagoon's north end.

We had just finished fueling a 99' aluminum crewboat at the commercial dock in Manzanillo and had planned to depart for San Diego. However in the brief 12 hours that we'd been in port, a mid-June tropical depression that had been southeast of us quickly became a hurricane and was steaming rapidly up the coast. It was projected to parallel the coast and pass well outside the harbor, and hopefully we'd catch only the edge of it.

We moved into the anchorage in the old port rather than the inner harbor. The steep hills to the southeast give protection to the harbor from the primary wind direction of an offshore storm. For 48 hours we stood anchor watch. The wind gusted and changed direction a few degrees as it alternately lined up in different gaps in the hills. But still it stayed in the southeast quadrant. We had gusts to 30 knots and much rain, but our anchor held tightly to Manzanillo's gooey bottom.

We could see across Manzanillo Bay toward the Las Hadas Marina, eight miles away. Huge waves were sweeping across the bay and crashing over the marina breakwater. Huge freighters anchored near there were pitching and rolling quite radically. Las Hadas definitely would not have been the place to be.

During this storm I could see the value of having some rope rode. Most of the boats I deliver have all chain ground tackle – as is common on the West Coast

66

and in coral seas. But this crew boat from the East Coast had 100 feet of chain and the rest rope rode. In severe gusty conditions a vessel will set strongly back on her anchor. In the case of chain, this shock can take all the catenary out of the chain until there is no give, and it will break the anchor out with a jerk, and you'll begin to drag. Rope stretches and acts as a buffer to prevent breaking the anchor's hold on the bottom. However chafe becomes a real problem with rope rode. You must have good chafing gear, stand constant watch on its condition, and be able to replace it immediately when necessary.

The hurricane roared by off shore and then turned west toward Hawaii. ("Harmlessly out to sea" as national TV weathermen frequently say. Obviously they don't go out to sea themselves.) We had survived this one because we had protection from the southeast. However Manzanillo often takes direct hits, and if that had been the case, we might have been better off in the inner harbor. Although it doesn't have as much protection from the hills to the southeast, at least it has more protection from shifting winds from other quadrants.

9. Lazaro Cardenas (17°55' North, 102°10' West)

Though it's a commercial harbor and not a place a pleasure boat might want to hang out, Lazaro Cardenas offers the best protection south of Puerto Vallarta. To ride out a hurricane, enter the port, proceed to the main turning basin, then turn right, go past the Pemex docks, and continue bearing right until you reach the undeveloped but deeply dredged channel basin. Anchor in 40 feet of water.

(In the past, cruisers used to seek a quick nap in Pesquera Basin, a small bay just to starboard immediately after you entered Lazaro Cardenas, but that basin is now developed by the Ports and Harbors Authority.)

Ixtapa is a slim possibility—but not good enough to qualify as a hurricane hole. Both of Marina Ixtapa's basins are landlocked but filled with slips. The Islas Blancas knock down some of the swell, and Cerro Ixtapa gives some shelter to the basins, and the marina's entrance channel (currently 7.5' deep) is slightly baffled. But the entrance faces almost due south, and it will quickly get closed out. Get in early.

Acapulco is another common hurricane target; don't linger here or anywhere south of here in the summer. Local boats at the Acapulco Yacht Club and La Marina survive because they are heavily moored; visitors might not be so lucky. Nearly 200 people died in and around Acapulco during the 1997 hurricane season. Municipal water supplies may be contaminated after storms.

Salina Cruz may be a surprise. A study of past hurricane tracks shows that Salina Cruz rarely lies in the danger path. The inner harbor is well protected but very crowded with commercial vessels.

10. Puerto Madero (14°42' North, 92°25' West)

Puerto Madero, like Salina Cruz, is rarely hit. The eastern basin has the best protection from swell. Puerto Madero is affected by local chubascos, however.

After leaving Acapulco early in October, 1997 aboard a 98' motoryacht we were taking from Seattle to Florida, we were hoping for a non-stop run to Panama. Eighteen hours out, a Tropical Depression formed 240 miles due south of us and was stationary. I wasn't unduly concerned because we were headed southeast, and hurricanes normally track northwest – which was away from us. Normally. But this El Nino year had been anything but normal and we'd already dodged three hurricanes since leaving San Diego.

Thirty six hours out, the T.D. had become Hurricane Pauline and she was headed east on a collision course with us. We were still 60 miles from Puerto Madero, which lies near the Guatemala border, when it became obvious that we had to seek shelter quickly. The wind quickly began to build to 25 knots on the nose. In these conditions I pushed the boat harder into a head sea than I normally would, because we needed to get into Madero's tricky little entrance channel before sunset, and I figured we'd just make it. I hand steered and tacked back and forth to avoid the biggest breaking crests, pulling back the throttles just before falling off a wave and then easing them forward in the relative "flat spots." The wind increased, the close seas built to eight feet, and the spindrift was just beginning to leave its white streaks of foam.

Four miles from Puerto Madero's breakwater, I called the "Capitania" (Port Captain's office) on VHF- 16 (Spanish only) to inform him of our arrival and that we were seeking shelter. Because they had been broadcasting hurricane warnings all afternoon, he said he thought coming is was a very good idea and was most helpful. I asked about bar conditions (rough) and where to anchor. He instructed me to anchor in the north basin and said that nobody else was anchored there, that all the shrimp boats where in the east basin, and to not worry about paper work until the storm was over.

Breakers were forming almost all the way across the entrance between the rip-rap breakwaters. I picked the calmest time I could and surfed in. In the failing light just after sunset, I saw a black buoy showing a green light and a tiny unlit red buoy. I passed through them with breakers to port and starboard, and then we were safely into calm waters. Puerto Madero is constantly shoaling in the entrance, and a dredge is permanently based there to keep it open.

As instructed I anchored in 40' off the fiscal wharf. True enough, we had the tiny basin all to ourselves and wouldn't have to worry about anybody dragging into us. However because the anchorage is so small, if we did drag we would drift into the mud almost immediately. Puerto Madero is nothing more that a dredged out mangrove swamp with low land all around it. However they have been dredging for many years and dumping the spoils on the land just southeast of us, which is the direction the wind was coming from. The pile was about 30' high and covered with scrub vegetation, which knocked down the wind considerably. We were now as secure as we could possibly be, and we stood continuous anchor watch—with alarms set on the GPS, radar and fathometer to immediately indicate any movement. We also stood constant radio watch.

Both the Navy and the Port Captain broadcast frequent updates on the storm, which in addition to my weather fax charts was quite helpful. Hurricane Pauline became a Category 4 hurricane with sustained winds of 115 knots. Fortunately for us, she recurved from her easterly track and headed north. At one point she was predicted to go ashore at Salina Cruz. I felt somewhat justified in my decision to go into Puerto Madero, because I had contemplated running off downwind back to Salina Cruz when the storm first formed. What actually happened was, Pauline continued turning northwest, raking the coastline, and eventually hit Acapulco— where we had been just five days before. She caused severe damage and loss of life.

We sat behind the mud pile for three nights while the storm never got closer that 120 miles, and we experienced maximum 25-knot gusts with rain, rain and more rain. All around us throughout the whole time, Mayan Indians stoically fished with hand lines from their dugout canoes, sometimes pathetically wrapping themselves up in plastic bags to keep out the rain.

Of all the hurricane holes, some have better round-the-compass wind shelter than do others, some have better holding ground than others, some have room to drag and soft places to drag into, some offer places to carry a line to shore, or a place to get survivors ashore. But in case of a direct hit, few boats can survive the violence of the wind and waves. Mexico's southern coast – so benign during the winter – is no place for ignorance in hurricane season; it could be fatal.

Hurricanes

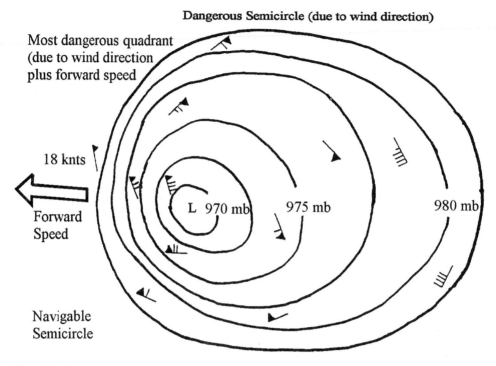

Dangerous Semicircle (due to wind direction)

Most dangerous quadrant (due to wind direction plus forward speed

18 knts

Forward Speed

L 970 mb   975 mb   980 mb

Navigable Semicircle

Fig. 24. Always maneuver to avoid the dangerous semicircle of a hurricane.

Some Definitions

Easterly waves: Wave-shaped stream lines superimposed upon the easterly winds in the Trade Wind belt. Their distinguishing feature is a trough of low pressure poking northward into the isobars of the Trade Winds, but you'll see no definite center of low pressure.

Tropical Depression: An area of low pressure with one or more closed isobars which has begun a counter-clockwise circulation. The highest sustained one-minute mean surface winds is 33 knots. Recognized tropical depressions are eventually given letters-numbers for names, such as TD-10.

Tropical Storm: An area of lower pressure with winds 34 to 63 knots. When it reaches this stage, the National Weather Service gives it an official name, such as Tropical Storm John.

Hurricane: An area of very low pressure with strongly pronounced counter-clockwise winds of 64 knots or higher. Hurricane John will probably be the upgraded form of Tropical Storm John.

Chubasco: This Spanish word is frequently misused by English speakers as synonymous with hurricane. Its correct definition is a violent thunderstorm occurring

May through October in the late afternoon and evening hours, sometimes several days in a row. Unlike hurricanes which develop over water, chubascos form in coastal mountains, then sweep out to sea. When being run over by a chubasco, you'll have wind beginning in the southwest, veering to the east to northeast, and then intensifying to gale force. Though chubascos can be severe, they are not as deadly as hurricanes because they are localized disturbances, lasting only a few hours and rarely raising a dangerous sea.

How to Maneuver to Avoid a Hurricane

Bowditch's "American Practical Navigator" gives what I feel is the best advice for emergency maneuvering to get out of the path of a nearby hurricane in the northern hemisphere:

1. Steer a course to put your boat in the NAVIGABLE SEMICIRCLE (Fig 24). The other side of the storm circle is even more dangerous, because wind speeds there will be augmented by the storm's forward movement. Hence, try to avoid the DANGEROUS SEMICIRCLE.

2. When your bow is directly into the wind, the storm's low-pressure center is to starboard (in the northern hemisphere) and somewhat to the rear. Plotting successive positions of the storm's center reveals which semicircle you're in.

3. If you're in the NAVIGABLE SEMICIRCLE, put the wind on your starboard quarter and make all haste away from the storm center.

4. If you're in the DANGEROUS SEMICIRCLE, put the wind on your starboard bow and make all haste away from the storm center.

5. Don't attempt to pass in front of the storm center, but if you must heave to in a sailing vessel within the DANGEROUS SEMICIRCLE, do so on a starboard tack.

Hurricanes

Chapter 9

MexWX Broadcasts

ᴜᴜᴜᴜᴜᴜᴜᴜᴜᴜᴜᴜᴜᴜᴜᴜᴜᴜᴜᴜᴜᴜᴜᴜ

W hen I'm presenting cruising seminars, I'm often asked, "What do we need aboard our boat in order to pick up weather reports while we're traveling in Mexican waters?"

Answer: Just some equipment and know-how.

To cruise or fish your way through Mexico, the bare minimum of equipment you'll require is a good receiver capable of picking up 1 to 22 MHz in the upper and lower side bands. Make it a transceiver, for 2-way communications. It should have high sensitivity and a good antenna with a tuner. A sailboat backstay can be rigged to make a good antenna for ham buffs, called Maritime Mobiles. Big power yachts usually carry everything, often in duplicate sets. It depends on how much space and money you decide to devote to equipment.

What about know-how? Considering how vital the weather is to the safety and happiness of boaters in Mexican waters, it's surprising how few of them know how and where to receive these important broadcasts, no matter how many gadgets they have. That's why I wrote this book.

Below you'll find information about the six basic types of marine weather reporting — VHF, HAM, SSB, WxFax, Internet, TV — available to boaters in Mexican waters. Each type has possibilities, so I've included the frequencies or channels and times you'll need in order to monitor weather reports for specific locations.

(1.) VHF RADIO

Very High Frequency (VHF) radio has a boat-to-boat range limited to only about 75 miles, depending on the antennae height. But occasionally VHF weather reports broadcast from San Diego can be heard as far south as Cedros Island. One segment of this weather report covers the offshore waters down to Guadalupe Island, so it's useful to travelers in Mexico's northern waters. VHF reports from other boats underway 50 miles ahead of you are very beneficial.

If you speak Spanish, you can generally get the latest local forecast by calling the local Port Captain's office on VHF-16. The larger ports broadcast weather reports in Spanish on a regular daily schedule, especially during hurricane season. These reports are given slowly and in simple Spanish.

Meteorological terms in Spanish can be found in the Appendices, as can the Beaufort Scale and many equivalent measures that are commonly used in Mexico.

(2.) HAM OR AMATEUR RADIO

I strongly recommend that boaters heading into Mexico carry HF radios capable of receiving ham frequencies on the lower side band, so they can monitor the weather-data gathering and forecasting portions of the ham networks, nets. (I also recommend that boaters get the ham license, so they can enjoy additional benefits, but having the ham-capable radio on board is a start.) Ham nets are the best method for gathering and disseminating news, and when it comes to news about immediate weather conditions, the best choice is:

CHUBASCO NET — The Chubasco Net provides the very best weather news in Mexican waters.

Frequency: 7294 kHz, LSB
Time: 0730 San Diego Time

Amateur radio operators check in and share their weather information from throughout Baja. Generally you cannot hear it south of Puerto Vallarta. The most useful of these reports come from vessels underway, but the reports from vessels at anchor are useful also. At 0745 the net forecaster gives his report. He gets his information from weather fax, and the early a.m. TV satellite pictures. He extrapolates these for the Baja area and combines them with the reports from vessels checking in.

You do not need to be licensed to listen to this net, but once you are you gain the greatest flexibility and service. After the forecaster gives his report, he calls for anyone with a weather question. At this point properly licensed amateur radio operators may ask specific questions pertinent to their area.

Even though this is the best information for Baja, this net (and others) gives it with a disclaimer: The net is in no way responsible for the consequences of any report or how any skipper uses the information.

(3.)   SSB or SINGLE SIDE BAND

Twelve Alpha (12353.0 MHz) is the ship-to-ship SSB channel regularly used by vessels off the coast of Baja, often passing reports of weather in their location, also water temperature and fishing news. Daily activity peaks around 1000 hours.

During cruising season, informal nets form on various other commercial SSB frequencies. These are generally used by cruisers without ham licenses to fill the function of ham nets. You can find out times and frequencies by listening to others talk about them on the ham nets. They come and go, so I don't list them here.

The Coast Guard Station NMC broadcasts National Weather Service (NWS) weather from San Francisco on a variety of frequencies receivable throughout Mexico. Except for tropical weather warnings and gale warnings for the Gulf of Tehuantepec, this reporting is so generalized that you'll have to draw your own forecast, depending on the positions of highs and lows given. The only specific forecast given is the same as the VHF report down to Guadalupe Island, mentioned above. KMI and WWV also give abbreviated forecasts as mentioned in the following schedules.

When speaking of the various SSB and WxFax stations, mariners use their phonetic identifiers, such as "November Mike Charlie" and "November Mike November," (not "en em see" and "en em en").

N6HOY and his ham rig at sea.

Explanatory notes to broadcasts:

1. Unless otherwise noted, all broadcast are Greenwich Mean Time, 24-hour clock (0000-2359). Frequencies listed are carrier frequencies.

2. Emission Classification is shown in parentheses immediately following the frequency. A3J—Single sideband, suppressed carrier.

3. Contents are indicated as follows:

A—Analysis
F—Forecast
P—Prognosis
S—Synopsis
SR—Synoptic reports
W—Warnings
G—Gulf Stream Analysis

Radio Costera
Spanish Only

Mexican weather is given in Spanish at 0930, 1530, and 2130 Central Standard Time over the national marine safety system called Radio Costera on SSB frequency 8242.8 kHz. The weather is for the entire Mexican coast by sections, and it's given by the various Port Captains throughout the country and it is very good. They deliver it slowly and clearly, so even with a modicum of Spanish, most boaters should be able to understand it. Because all the Port Captains throughout the country are listening in, it makes a great emergency calling frequency.

National Bureau of Standards. Fort Collins, CO   # WWV

Broadcast from Colorado and Hawaii, this SSB station's primary function is giving the "time tick," which is indispensable for accurate navigation at sea, but it also gives abbreviated Pacific weather at 10 minutes past each hour. The WWV report is limited to severe weather warnings such as gales in the Gulf of Tehuantepec and elsewhere, tropical depressions, tropical storms, and hurricanes. It is also a source of checking radio propogation conditions and the latest status of the GPS navigation system.

Broadcast Time	Frequency (kHz) (A3)
H+10	5000
	10000
	15000

U.S.C.G. San Francisco   **NMC**

Area:

(a) North Pacific, Equator to 30°N, east of 140°W.

(b) North Pacific, north of 30°N, east of 160°E.

(c) Offshore Waters, 20 to 250 miles from shore, Mexican Border-Cape Flattery, Wash.

Broadcast Time (UTC)	Frequency (Khz) (A3J)	Channel	Contents
0430, 1030	4426	424	W, F
	8764	816	
	13089	1205	
1630, 2230	8764	816	
	13089	1205	
	17314	1625	

A voice weather broadcast can be confusing until you have heard the complex format several times. The following is the text of a complete voice forecast in the exact order given by NMC. I have highlighted the sections that sometimes contain information pertinent to Mexico, so you should be listening for them. Note how little information is available. Other than ham radio reports and your own interpretation of weather faxes, this is all you'll have.

HIGH SEAS FORECAST
TROPICAL ANALYSIS AND FORECAST BRANCH
TROPICAL PREDICTION CENTER MIAMI FL
1630 UTC TUE DEC 09 1997

E PACIFIC FROM THE EQUATOR TO 30N E OF 140W.
SYNOPSIS VALID 1200 UTC TUE DEC 09.
FORECAST VALID 0000 UTC THU DEC 11.
WARNINGS...
NONE.
SYNOPSIS AND FORECAST...
1200 UTC DEC 09...RIDGE N OF 15N W OF 110W. FORECAST

0000 UTC DEC 11...LITTLE CHANGE.

1200 UTC DEC 09...N OF 10N BETWEEN 110W AND 125W WIND N TO NE 20 KT SEAS 8 TO 10 FT IN NW SWELL. N OF 15N BETWEEN 125W AND 133W WIND NE TO E 20 TO 25 KT SEAS 8 TO 12 FT IN NE SWELL. N OF 15N W OF 133W WIND E TO SE 20 TO 25 KT SEAS 8 TO 12 FT IN N SWELL. FORECAST 0000 UTC DEC 11...LITTLE CHANGE.

REMAINDER AREA WINDS LESS THAN 20 KT SEAS LESS THAN 8 FT THROUGH 0000 UTC DEC 11.
...
CONVECTION VALID AS OF 1500 UTC TUE DEC 09...
INTERTROPICAL CONVERGENCE ZONE...AXIS 2N82W 5N105W 8N112W 2N123W 5N130W 2N140W. NUMEROUS MODERATE AND STRONG WITHIN 90 NM 5N80W. WIDELY SCATTERED MODERATE AND ISOLATED STRONG WITHIN 90 NM OF AXIS BETWEEN 84W AND 98W...AND FROM 109W TO 122W.

SECURITE
PACIFIC N OF 30N AND E OF A LINE FROM THE BERING STRAIT TO 160E. SYNOPSIS VALID 1200 UTC 28 DEC 97. FORECAST VALID 0000 UTC 30 DEC 97

WARNINGS

DEVELOPING STORM 34N 159E 994 MB MOVING NE 25 KT. WINDS 35 TO 45 KT SEAS 16 TO 24 FT FROM 29N TO 38N W OF 167E. BY 0000 UTC 29 DEC STORM 38N 164E 982 MB WITH WINDS 35 TO 50 KT SEAS 18 TO 28 FT WITHIN 480 NM E SEMI-CIRCLE AND WITHIN 240 NM W QUADRANT.
FORECAST STORM 52N 172E 974 MB WITH FRONT FROM CEN-TER TO 45N 179E. FORECAST WINDS 45 TO 60 KT SEAS 24 TO 34 FT WITHIN 300 NM N OF FRONT. ELSEWHERE FORECAST WINDS 30 TO 45 KT SEAS 18 TO 26 FT WITHIN 600 NM E SEMI-CIRCLE AND SW QUADRANT.

DEVELOPING STORM 51N 160E 985 MB MOVING N 15 KT.

WINDS 30 TO 45 KT SEAS 12 TO 22 FT N OF 41N W OF 168E.

OFFSHORE WATERS FORECAST
NATIONAL WEATHER SERVICE WASHINGTON DC
MARINE PREDICTION CENTER/MARINE FORECAST BRANCH
830 AM PST SUN DEC 28 1997
CALIFORNIA WATERS FROM 60 NM TO 250 NM OFFSHORE
SYNOPSIS...HIGH PRES NEAR 40N 130W WILL REMAIN STATIONARY THROUGH MON WITH A TROUGH DEVELOPING ALONG THE COAST S OF PT ARENA.
POINT ST GEORGE TO POINT ARENA
TODAY... NW PORTION...VARIABLE WINDS 10 KT. SEAS 7 TO 10 FT. SE PORTION...NE WINDS 10 TO 20 KT. SEAS 7 TO 10 FT. TONIGHT...NW PORTION...VARIABLE WINDS 10 KT. SEAS 7 TO 10 FT. SE PORTION...NE WINDS 10 TO 20 KT. SEAS 7 TO 10 FT..MON...NE WINDS 10 TO 15 KT. SEAS 6 TO 9 FT.

POINT ARENA TO POINT CONCEPTION

TODAY...NE WINDS 10 TO 20 KT. SEAS 7 TO 10 FT.
TONIGHT...NE WINDS 10 TO 20 KT. SEAS 7 TO 10 FT.
MON...NE WINDS 10 TO 15 KT. SEAS 6 TO 9 FT.

POINT CONCEPTION TO GUADALUPE ISLAND

TODAY... NE WINDS 10 TO 20 KT. SEAS 7 TO 10 FT EXCEPT 5 FT E OF 120W. TONIGHT...NE WINDS 10 TO 20 KT. SEAS 7 TO 10 FT EXCEPT 5 FT E OF 120W. MON...NE WINDS 10 TO 15 KT. SEAS 6 TO 9 FT EXCEPT 5 FT E OF 120W.
MARINE EXTENDED OUTLOOK FOR CALIFORNIA WATERS SOUTH TO GUADALUPE ISLAND

MON NIGHT THROUGH THU...HIGH PRES RIDGE WILL CONTINUE ACROSS THE NORTHERN WATERS THROUGH TUE THEN DRIFT S WED AND THU. A COLD FRONT WILL MOVE INTO THE AREA FROM THE W WED NIGHT AND THU. GALE FORCE WINDS..

USCG Master Station Atlantic, Chesapeake, Virginia   **NMN**
Simulcast on NMG, easier to receive in Mexico. See page 87.

Area:

(a)The National Weather Service forecast for the offshore waters consists of the west central North Atlantic offshore waters between 32° North and 41° North and West of 65° West, the southwest North Atlantic, the Gulf of Mexico, and the Caribbean Sea and, with the exception of the 0330 UTC broadcast, the offshore waters east of New England north of 41° North and west of 60° West. The offshore forecasts are given at :

Broadcast Time (UTC)	Frequency (kz) (A3J)	Channel
0330, 0930	4426	424
	6501	601
	8764	816
1600, 2200	6501	601
	8764	816
	13089	1205

(b) The high seas forecast consists of the North Atlantic waters north of 03° North and west of 35° West including the Gulf of Mexico the Caribbean Sea. The high seas forecast is given at:

Broadcast Time (UTC)	Frequency (kHz) (A3J)	Channel
0500	4426	424
	6501	601
	8764	816
1130, 2330	6501	601
	8764	816
	13089	1205
1730	8764	816
	13089	1205
	17314	1625

Area (a) has the most thorough forecast.

(4.) WxFAX or WEATHER FAX

Weather fax is simply a specialized SSB receiver that prints out weather charts. Each year, newer models of this onboard device get more sophisticated and less expensive. Station NMC (San Francisco) broadcasts for Mexico. While its reports are better than voice broadcasts, most charts cover such a wide area that valuable data specific to Mexico is scanty. From Puerto Vallarta south, you'll be wise to also receive NMG from New Orleans and reception is good. NMC's satellite photos do not cover the Mexican mainland south of Puerto Vallarta and NMG does. In fact even in Baja and the Sea of Cortez you'll need NMG's satellite photos during hurricane season in order to see what is going on farther south. Moreover, even though NMG is primarily for the Gulf of Mexico and Caribbean, it also has chart coverage on the Pacific side of Mexico. Besides, much of southern Mexico's weather is influenced by what is happening on the other side. Use NAM as an East Coast back up. This Navy station's transmitter is in Culter, Maine and not nearly as easy to pick up as NMG.

If you already have an all-band receiver built into your radio and have an onboard computer, you can have weather-fax capabilities without much additional expense. One firm I know of sells a software package with a small modem to link the radio and computer in order to receive weather faxes. Their package sells for about $179.95. Contact Software Systems Consulting, 150 Avenida Cabrillo, San Clemente, CA 92672. (949) 498-0568.

Weather-fax stations located around the US broadcast a huge variety of charts, which they call "products," for many different purposes, not always relevant to boaters. This variety can be confusing to the novice, causing him or her to waste rolls and rolls of expensive fax paper on irrelevant charts. So I've listed here the frequencies of my favorite WxFax stations — along with the stars on titles of that station's most useful charts, starting with those that pertain to portions of Mexico and moving down through Panama.

In Baja and the Sea of Cortez, you'll need to run two kinds of charts; first, for upper California, since that affects what happens farther south; also, the tropical surface analysis. From Puerto Vallarta south you can drop California and just run NMC's tropical analysis plus NMG's charts and photos. A routine of receiving one round of starred charts per day should be adequate. In unsettled weather you should run a round at least twice a day.

The exact time of day that each particular chart is broadcast has been changing several times a year. However, each station does broadcast its own "Fax Schedule" telling us when to tune in for which charts, and that should be accurate for several months, before it changes again. The time the Fax Schedule is broadcast has not changed so I included that. You need to first receive the most recent Fax Schedule to check for the current times of these "products," then you can stand-by for only those charts you need.

SAN DIEGO TO PUERTO VALLARTA

PT. REYES, CALIFORNIA, U.S.A. (SAN FRANCISCO)   **NMC**

CALL SIGN	FREQUENCIES	TIMES	EMISSION	POWER
NMC	4346 kHz	NIGHT	F3C	10 KW
	8682 kHz	CONTINUOUS	F3C	10 KW
	12730 kHz	CONTINUOUS	F3C	10 KW
	17151.2 kHz	CONTINUOUS	F3C	10 KW
	22527 kHz	DAY	F3C	10 KW

TRANS TIME	CONTENTS OF TRANSMISSION	VALID TIME	MAP AREA
0245/1430	TEST PATTERN		
0248/1438	SATELLITE IMAGE	LATEST	7/5
0259/1449	SATELLITE IMAGE	LATEST	5/6
0310/1500	SEA STATE ANALYSIS	00/12	1/8
——/1510	0/24HR WIND/SEAS FORECAST (2 CHARTS)	12&12	4
0320/1520	SURFACE ANALYSIS (PART 1 NE PACIFIC)	00/12	2
0333/1533	SURFACE ANALYSIS (PART 2 NW PACIFIC)	00/12	3
0345/1545	500MB ANALYSIS	00/12	1
0355/1555	(REBROADCAST OF 0320/1520)	00/12	2
0408/1608	(REBROADCAST OF 0333/1533)	00/12	3
0800/1930	TEST PATTERN		
0808/1933	24HR SURFACE FORECAST	00/12	8
0818/1943	24HR WIND/WAVE FORECAST	00/12	8
0828/1953	48HR 500MB FORECAST	00/12	1
0838/2003	48HR SURFACE FORECAST	00/12	1
0848/2013	48HR WIND/WAVE FORECAST	00/12	1
0858/2023	48HR WAVE PERIOD FORECAST	00/12	1
——/2033	96 HR 500MB FORECAST	0000	1
——/2043	96 HR SURFACE FORECAST	0000	1
——/2053	96 HR WIND/WAVE FORECAST	0000	1
——/2103	96 HR WAVE PERIOD FORECAST	0000	1
0908/2113	SATELLITE IMAGE	06/18	7/5
0919/2124	SURFACE ANALYSIS (PART 1 NE PACIFIC)	06/18	2
0932/2137	SURFACE ANALYSIS (PART 2 NW PACIFIC)	06/18	3
0944/——	SATELLITE IMAGE	0600	5
——/2149	0/24HR WIND/SEAS FORECAST (2 CHARTS)	18&18	4
0955/2159	(REBROADCAST OF 0919/2124)	06/18	2
1008/2212	(REBROADCAST OF 0932/2137)	06/18	3
1100/2300	TEST PATTERN		
——/2304	SST ANALYSIS	LATEST	9
——/2314	SST ANALYSIS	LATEST	6
1104/2324	*BROADCAST SCHEDULE (PART 1)*		
1115/2335	*BROADCAST SCHEDULE (PART 2)*		

MexWX Broadcasts

A Sample of NMC Products

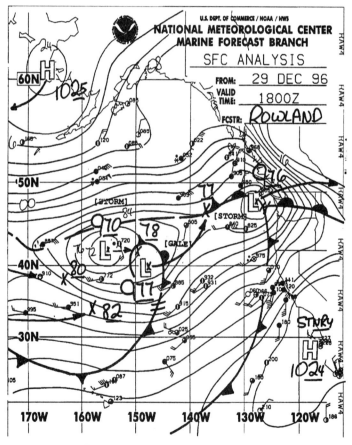

Fig. 25. Vessels in northern Baja should
pick up NMC's surface analysis.

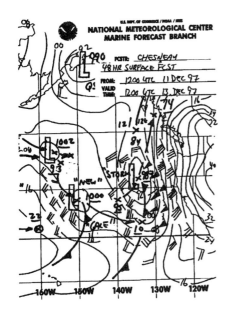

Fig. 26. Northern Baja vessels will find NMC's 48-hour prognosis useful for forecasting. The station also has a 24-hour prognosis.

Fig. 27. The tropical analysis from NMC is the most useful for skippers in Mexico.

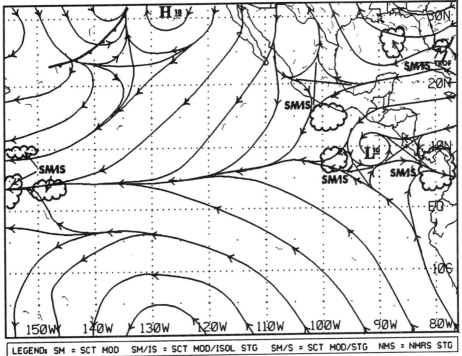

LEGEND: SM = SCT MOD   SM/IS = SCT MOD/ISOL STG   SM/S = SCT MOD/STG   NMS = NMRS STG

EAST PACIFIC SURFACE ANALYSIS   TROPICAL PREDICTION CENTER / TAFB
NATIONAL HURRICANE CENTER
VALID: 12Z MAY 30 1997   MIAMI, FLORIDA   33165-2149
ANALYST: cab   305-229-4470

Fig. 28. For satellite coverage as far as Puerto Vallarta, use NMC (above).
Fig. 29. During hurricane season also use NMG's satellite (below) in order
to see what is forming farther southeast along the Mexican coast.

PUERTO VALLARTA TO PANAMA

NEW ORLEANS, LOUISIANA, U.S.A.

NMG

CALL SIGN	FREQUENCIES	TIMES	EMISSION	POWER
NMG	4317.9 kHz	CONTINUOUS	F3C	10 KW
	8503.9 kHz	CONTINUOUS	F3C	10 KW
	12789.9 kHz	CONTINUOUS	F3C	10 KW

TRANS TIME	CONTENTS OF TRANSMISSION	VALID TIME	MAP AREA
0000/*1200	TROPICAL SURFACE ANALYSIS	18/06	1
0030/*1230	24/36 HR WIND/SEAS FORECAST (2 CHARTS)	00&12/12&00	2
0050/*1250	HIGH SEAS FORECAST (IN ENGLISH)	22/10	5
0115/*1315	0/12 HR WIND/SEAS FORECAST (2 CHARTS)	00&12/12&00	2
0135/*1335	U.S. SURFACE ANALYSIS	18/06	3
0150/*1350	GOES-8 IR TROPICAL SATELLITE IMAGE	2345/1145	4
0205/1405	REQUEST FOR COMMENTS/PRODUCT NOTICE		
0600/1800	TROPICAL SURFACE ANALYSIS	00/12	1
0630/1830	*BROADCAST SCHEDULE*		
0650/1850	HIGH SEAS FORECAST (IN ENGLISH)	04/16	5
0715/1915	0/12 HR WIND/SEAS FORECAST (2 CHARTS)	06&18/18&06	2
0735/1935	U.S. SURFACE ANALYSIS	00/12	3
0750/1950	GOES-8 IR TROPICAL SATELLITE IMAGE	0645/1745	4
0805/2005	(REBROADCAST OF 0030/1230)	00&12/12&00	2

NOTES: 1. CARRIER FREQUENCY IS 1.9 kHz BELOW THE ASSIGNED FREQUENCY
          2. THIS BROADCAST ORIGINATES FROM THE TROPICAL PREDICTION CENTER

<u>MAP AREAS:</u>
1. 05S - 35N,   0 - 120W
2. 10N - 30N, 55W - 100W
3. 15N - 50N, 65W - 125W
4. 12S - 44N, 28W - 112W
5. 3N - 32N, 35W - 100W

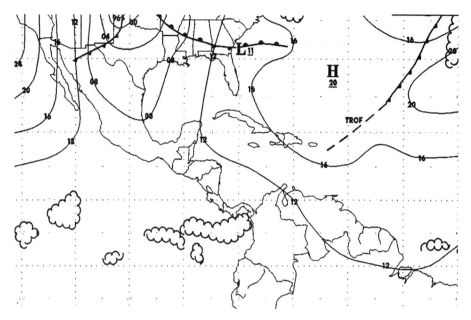

Fig. 30. With coverage from Southern California to Africa, NMG's tropical analysis is indispensible in Mexico.

A Sample of NMG Products

Fig. 31. In a two-panel series NMG shows the 24-36-hour forecast. The station also has the same format for current and 12-hour forecasts. Even though its primary focus is for the Gulf of Mexico and Caribbean, it is also very useful in the Pacific.

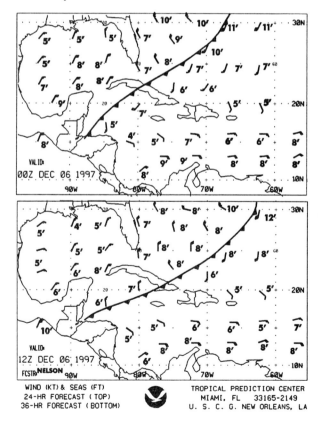

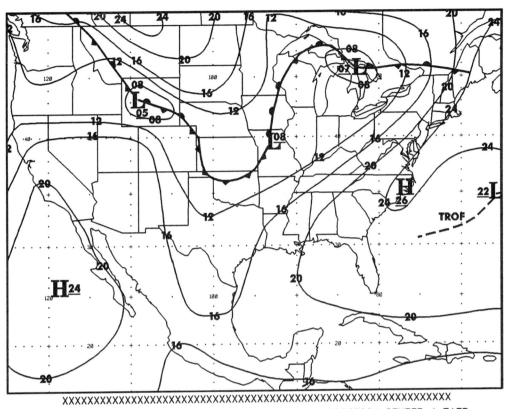

XXXXXXXXXXXXXXXXXXXXXXXXXXXXXXXXXXXXXXXXXXXXXXXXXXXXXXXXXXXXX
NORTH AMERICAN SURFACE ANALYSIS   TROPICAL PREDICTION CENTER / TAFB
VALID: 18Z DEC 28 1996   NATIONAL HURRICANE CENTER
ANALYST: FORMOSA   MIAMI, FLORIDA   33165-2149
    U. S. COAST GUARD   305-229-4470
  BELLE CHASE, LOUISIANA
XXXXXXXXXXXXXXXXXXXXXXXXXXXXXXXXXXXXXXXXXXXXXXXXXXXXXXXXXXXXX

Fig. 32. For the big picture, use NMG's North
American Surface Analysis.

(5.) INTERNET

http://weather.noaa.gov/fax/marine.html.

All of the above charts of the stations listed above can be downloaded from the internet. In the not too distant future all cruising boats will have satellite links to the internet. As a matter of fact, most internet charts are much clearer and show more detail than faxes transmitted by HF radio. In the meantime, if you don't have weather fax on your boat, if you're planning a cruise and have access to the internet, check out this website and download the charts. With a little bit of familiarity, you'll get used to what these products are like and what they mean.

At the above website, you just click on the charts you want and download them. However this method is slow, and sometimes the charts come in defective. It's much faster and more effective to use the ftp (file transfer protocol) transfer. On the homepage click on the highlighted "FTP" and you'll be presented with a list of chart file names. Use the cross reference lists on the following pages to click on your chart. You can also download this list from the site. Then download the chart. It's a good idea to rename the chart something useful that you can recognize – other than an esoteric group of letters and numbers.

The above website contains many links to other useful weather websites such as interactive buoy reports and surface observations in Mexico.

Marine Charts on the NET

The *latest version* of marine weather charts for broadcast by the U.S. Coast Guard are available from the National Weather Service Telecommunication Gateway on this server. The listed charts are in the G4 (T4) format and enveloped in TIFF for viewing.

If this http server is ever busy, or errors occur in downloading try the anonymous FTP server - ftp://www.nws.noaa.gov/fax

These products also available via E-mail

Caution

The Charts are organized according to broadcast areas

Select the broadcast area

Atlantic | Pacific | Gulf of Mexico

Alaska | Hawaii

RADIOFAX RELATED LINKS

NWS Marine and Satellite Products
Marine Prediction Center
Tropical Prediction Center
Voluntary Observing Ships Program
Shipboard Environmental Acquisition System(SEAS)
U.S. Coast Guard Navigation Center
Ship & Buoy Observations from Penn State
The Radiofacsimile WWW Page
International Ice Patrol
NOAA CNODDS
Naval Oceanographic Office
Navy Fleet Numerical
Marine Weather from Ohio State

Go To NWS Welcome Page... Go to Frequently Asked Questions Page... Go To Search Page... Go To Feedback Page...
Author: *Cliff Fridlind*, NWS Office of Systems Operations

National Oceanic and Atmospheric AdministrationNational Weather Service
Last Modified: Thursday, 23-Oct-97 13:27:58

Fig. 33. The home webpage for Marine Weather Charts on the Net leads to NMC (Pacific), NMG (Atlantic) as well as other sites of interest to the mariner.

NATIONAL WEATHER SERVICE RADIOFAX PRODUCTS
for the Eastern Pacific Ocean
The latest version of marine weather charts for broadcast by the U.S. Coast
Guard are available from the National Weather Service Telecommunication
Gateway on this server. The listed charts are in the G4(T4) format and
enveloped in TIFF for viewing. These charts may be found in directory:
ftp://www.weather.noaa.gov/fax

WIND/SEAS CHARTS	FILE NAMES
00Z Sea State Analysis 115W-155W Northern Hemisphere;	PWBA88.TIF
12Z Sea State Analysis 115W-155W Northern Hemisphere;	PWBA89.TIF
Sea State Analysis (Most Current)	PWBA90.TIF
24HR Wind/Seas Forecast VT00Z Forecast 115W-155W N. Hemisphere;	PWBE98.TIF
24HR Wind/Seas Forecast VT12Z Forecast 115W-155W N. Hemisphere;	PWBE99.TIF
24HR Wind/Seas Forecast (Most Current);	PWBE10.TIF
48HR Sea Surface Chart VT00Z Forecast 115W-135E N. Hemisphere;	PJBI98.TIF
48HR Sea Surface Chart VT12Z Forecast 115W-135E N. Hemisphere;	PJBI99.TIF
48HR Sea Surface Chart (Most Current);	PJBI10.TIF

SURFACE CHARTS	
00Z Surface Chart Analysis 115W-175W N. Hemisphere (Part 1);	PYBA01.TIF
00Z Surface Chart Analysis 175W-135E N. Hemisphere (Part 2);	PYBA02.TIF
06Z Surface Chart Analysis 115W-175W N. Hemisphere (Part 1);	PYBA03.TIF
06Z Surface Chart Analysis 175W-135E N. Hemisphere (Part 2);	PYBA04.TIF
12Z Surface Chart Analysis 115W-175W N. Hemisphere (Part 1);	PYBA05.TIF
12Z Surface Chart Analysis 175W-135E N. Hemisphere (Part 2);	PYBA06.TIF
18Z Surface Chart Analysis 115W-175W N. Hemisphere (Part 1);	PYBA07.TIF
18Z Surface Chart Analysis 175W-135E N. Hemisphere (Part 2);	PYBA08.TIF
Surface Chart Analysis, Part 1 (Most Current);	PYBA11.TIF
Surface Chart Analysis, Part 2 (Most Current);	PYBA12.TIF
12Z Eastern Pacific Streamline Analysis 80W-160W N. Hemisphere;	PGBA00.TIF
18Z Eastern Pacific Streamline Analysis 80W-160W N. Hemisphere;	PGBA01.TIF
Eastern Pacific Streamline Analysis (Most Current);	PGBA10.TIF
24HR Surface Chart VT00Z Forecast 115W-155W N. Hemisphere;	PPBE00.TIF
24HR Surface Chart VT12Z Forecast 115W-155W N. Hemisphere;	PPBE01.TIF
24HR Surface Chart Forecast (Most Current);	PPBE10.TIF
48HR Surface Chart VT00Z Forecast 115W-135E N. Hemisphere;	PWBI98.TIF
48HR Surface Chart VT12Z Forecast 115W-135E N. Hemisphere;	PWBI99.TIF
48HR Surface Chart Forecast (Most Current);	PWBI10.TIF

UPPER AIR CHARTS

00Z 500 MB Analysis 115W-135E Northern Hemisphere;	PPBA50.TIF
12Z 500 MB Analysis 115W-135E Northern Hemisphere;	PPBA51.TIF
500 MB Analysis (Most Current);	PPBA10.TIF
48HR 500 MB Chart VT00Z Forecast 115W-135E Northern Hemisphere;	PPBI50.TIF
48HR 500 MB Chart VT12Z Forecast 115W-135E Northern Hemisphere;	PPBI51.TIF
500 MB Chart Forecast (Most Current);	PPBI10.TIF
96HR 500MB CHART VT00Z 115W-135E Northern Hemisphere;	PPBM50.TIF

SEA SURFACE TEMPERATURES

Pacific SST Chart 115W-135W;	PTBA88.TIF
Pacific SST Chart 105W-130W;	PTBA89.TIF

SATELLITE IMAGERY

00Z GOES-7 Infrared	EVPN00.JPG
01Z GOES-7 Infrared	EVPN01.JPG
06Z GOES-7 Infrared	EVPN06.JPG
07Z GOES-7 Infrared	EVPN07.JPG
12Z GOES-7 Infrared	EVPN12.JPG
13Z GOES-7 Infrared	EVPN13.JPG
18Z GOES-7 Infrared	EVPN18.JPG
19Z GOES-7 Infrared	EVPN19.JPG
GOES-7 Infrared (MOST CURRENT)	EVPN99.JPG

Note: GOES satellite imagery sent via radiofax is not currently
available on this Web Site for technical reasons.

SCHEDULE INFORMATION

Radiofax Schedule Part 1 (Point Reyes, CA);	PLBZ01.TIF
Radiofax Schedule Part 2 (Point Reyes, CA);	PLBZ02.TIF
Radiofax Schedule (DOS Text Format);	hfreyes.txt
Request for Comments;	PLBZ03.TIF
Product Notice Bulletin;	PLBZ04.TIF
Test Pattern;	PZZZ93.TIF

MexWX Broadcasts

NATIONAL WEATHER SERVICE RADIOFAX PRODUCTS
for the Gulf of Mexico and Tropical Atlantic
U.S. Coast Guard Communications Station NMG - New Orleans, Louisiana
The latest version of marine weather charts for broadcast by the U.S. Coast
Guard are available from the National Weather Service Telecommunication
Gateway on this server. The listed charts are in the G4(T4) format and
enveloped in TIFF for viewing. These charts may be found in directory:
ftp://www.nws.noaa.gov/fax

WIND/SEAS CHARTS	FILE NAMES
00/24HR Wind/Seas Forecast (2 Charts) VT06/06Z;	PYEA96.TIF
00/24HR Wind/Seas Forecast (2 Charts) VT12/12Z;	PYEA97.TIF
00/24HR Wind/Seas Forecast (2 Charts) VT18/18Z;	PYEA98.TIF
00/24HR Wind/Seas Forecast (2 Charts) VT00/00Z;	PYEA99.TIF
00/24HR Wind/Seas Forecast (Most Current);	PYEA10.TIF
48/72HR Wind/Seas Forecast (2 Charts) VT00/00Z;	PWED98.TIF
48/72HR Wind/Seas Forecast (2 Charts) VT12/12Z;	PWED99.TIF
48/72HR Wind/Seas Forecast (Most Current);	PWED10.TIF

SURFACE CHARTS

U.S. Surface Chart Analysis at 00Z Continental U.S.;	PYAA98.TIF
U.S. Surface Chart Analysis at 06Z Continental U.S.;	PYAA97.TIF
U.S. Surface Chart Analysis at 12Z Continental U.S.;	PYAA99.TIF
U.S. Surface Chart Analysis at 18Z Continental U.S.;	PYAA96.TIF
U.S. Surface Chart Analysis (Most Current);	PYAA20.TIF
Tropical Surface Chart Analysis at 00Z;	PYEA86.TIF
Tropical Surface Chart Analysis at 06Z;	PYEA87.TIF
Tropical Surface Chart Analysis at 12Z;	PYEA85.TIF
Tropical Surface Chart Analysis at 18Z;	PYEA88.TIF
Tropical Surface Chart Analysis (Most Current);	PYEA11.TIF

HIGH SEAS FORECASTS

04Z High Seas Forecast 0-90W Tropical Belt, TEXT DOCUMENT;	PLEA86.TIF
10Z High Seas Forecast 0-90W Tropical Belt, TEXT DOCUMENT;	PLEA87.TIF
16Z High Seas Forecast 0-90W Tropical Belt, TEXT DOCUMENT;	PLEA89.TIF
22Z High Seas Forecast 0-90W Tropical Belt, TEXT DOCUMENT;	PLEA88.TIF
High Seas Forecast (Most Current);	PLEA10.TIF

SATELLITE IMAGERY

0645Z GOES-8 Tropical Infrared	EVST06.JPG
1145Z GOES-8 Tropical Infrared	EVST12.JPG
1745Z GOES-8 Tropical Infrared	EVST18.JPG
2345Z GOES-8 Tropical Infrared	EVST00.JPG
GOES-8 Tropical Infrared (Most Current);	EVST99.JPG

Note: GOES satellite imagery sent via radiofax is not currently
available on this Web Site for technical reasons.

SCHEDULE INFORMATION

Radiofax Schedule (New Orleans, LA);	PLEZ01.TIF
Radiofax Schedule (DOS Text Format);	hfgulf.txt
Request for Comments;	PLEZ02.TIF
Product Notice Bulletin;	PLEZ03.TIF
Internet File Names (Gulf of Mexico)	rfaxmex.txt

Document URL: http://tgsv5.nws.noaa.gov/pub/fax/rfaxmex.txt

(6.) TELEVISION

The Weather Channel. Although very few boats are equipped with satellite TV, many marinas in Mexico such as Marina Vallarta have cable TV with The Weather Channel. In other larger cities, you can at least find a hotel lobby or bar with TWC available. You'll find it very useful if you are holed up for weather and planning to jump off on the next leg, especially during the hurricane season.

The Tropical Weather Update at 10 minutes before each hour is invaluable. Its satellite photos in motion tell you much more than still satellite pictures downloaded on weather fax. They also have valuable information about possibilities of future developments and tracks.

In past years, TWC Tropical Update focused primarily on the US Eastern Seaboard, especially around Atlanta, where the program originates. After El Niño began kicking up weather storms in the Pacific, the TV weather people have began learning a few new place names on Mexico's West Coast - but they still confuse Manzanillo with Mazatlán.

MexWX Broadcasts

Spanish Meteorological Terms

wwwwwwwwwwwwww

Approach (to): acercar
Barometer: barómetro
Breakers: rompientes
Breeze: brisa
       light: brisa muy debil
       gentle: brisa moderada
       fresh: brisa fresca
       strong: brisa fuerte
Calm: calma
Clear (to): aclarar
Cloud: nube
Degrees: grados
Depression: depresión
East: este, oriente
Ebb tide: marea menguantes
Forecast: predición
Fog: niebla
Front: frente
Gale: viento duro
GMT: hora media de Greenwich
Gust: rafaga, racha
Haze: bruma
High pressure: alta presión
Horizon: horizonte

Hurricane: huracán
Knots: nudos
Light airs: ventorinas
Lightning: relámpago
Mist: neblina
North: norte
Norther: nortada
Rain: lluvia
Sea: mar
Showers: chubascos
South: sur
Squall: turbonada
Storm: temporál
Surf: marejada, resaca
Surge: olejada, resaca
Swell: mar de fondo
Thunder: trueño
Tide: marea
Trade Winds: vientos alisos
Tropical cyclone: ciclón tropical
Tropical depression: perturbación tropical
Waves: olas
Weather: tiempo
West: oeste, poniente

Beaufort Scale

Beaufort Number	Mean Velocity Knots	Descriptive Term	Deep Sea Criterion	Wave Height in Feet
0	< 1	Calm	Sea like a mirror	
1	1-3	Light	Ripples with the appearance of scales are formed but without foam crests.	.25
2	4-6	Light Breeze	Small Wavelets, still short but more pronounced. Crests have a glassy appearance	.5-1
3	7-10	Gentle Breeze	Large wavelets. Crests begin to break. Foam of glassy appearance. Perhaps scattered white horses.	2-3
4	11-16	Moderate Breeze	Small waves, become longer; fairly frequent horses	3.5-5
5	17-21	Fresh Breeze	Moderate waves, taking a more pronounced long form; many white horses formed. Chance of some spray.	6-8.5
6	22-27	Strong Breeze	Large waves begin to form; the white foam crests are more extensive everywhere. Probably some spray.	9.5-13

Beaufort Number	Mean Velocity Knots	Descriptive Term	Deep Sea Criterion	Wave Height in Feet
7	28-33	Near Gale	Sea heaps up and white foam from breaking waves begins to be blown in streaks along the direction of the wind.	13.5-19
8	34-40	Gale	Moderately high waves of greater length; edges of crest begin to break into spindrift. The foam is blown in well-marked streaks along the direction of the wind.	18-25
9	41-47	Strong Gale	High waves. Dense streaks of foam along the direction of the wind. Crest of waves begin to topple, tumble and roll over. Spray may affect visibility.	23-32
10	48-55	Storm	Very high waves with long overhanging crest. The resulting foam in great patches is blown in dense white streaks along the direction of the wind. On the whole, the surface of the sea takes a white appearance. The tumbling of the sea becomes heavy and shocklike. Visibility affected.	29-41
11	58-63	Violent Storm	Exceptionally high waves. Small and medium sized ships might be for a time lost to view behind the waves. The sea is completely covered with long white patches of foam lying along the direction of the wind. Everywhere the ridges of the wave's crest are blown into froth. Visibility affected.	37-52
12	63+	Hurricane	The air is filled with foam and spray. Sea completely white with driving spray; visibility very seriously affected.	45+

Equivalent Measures

~~~~~~~~~~~~~~~~~~~~~~~~~~~~~

Linear
1 Kilometer = 1000 meters = 3280 feet = .54 naut. mile = .62 stat. mile
1 Meter = 3.28 feet = 39.37 inches
1 Degree of Latitude = 111.1 kilometers

Capacity
1 Liter = .265 U.S. gallons = 61.02 cubic inches

Velocity
1 Mile per hour = 1.467 feet per second = .447 meters per second = 1.61 kilometers per hour = .868 knot
1 Meter per second = 3.6 kilometers per hour = 1.94 knots
1 Knot = 1.152 miles per hour = 1.854 kilometers per hour = .515 meters per second

Pressure
Millibars = Inches x 33.865

$$\text{Inches} = \frac{\text{Millibars}}{33.865}$$

1 Millimeter Mercury = .03937 inch = 1.3332 Millibars

Temperature

Celsius = Centigrade
Centigrade = 5/9(Fahrenheit -32)
Fahrenheit = 9/5 Centigrade + 32

Appendix D

Bibliography

ᴜᴜᴜᴜᴜᴜᴜᴜᴜᴜᴜᴜᴜᴜᴜᴜᴜᴜᴜᴜᴜᴜᴜᴜᴜᴜᴜᴜᴜᴜ

———.*Atlas de Huracanes,* Secretaria de Porgamación y Presupuesto, Mexico, D.F.

Crawford, William, *Mariner's Weather, W.W. Norton, New York, 1992.*

Bishop, Joseph Dr., *A Mariner's Guide to Radio Facsimile Weather Charts,* Alden Electronics, Westborough, MA, 1984.

Kraght, Peter, *Meteorology for Ship and Aircraft Operation,* Cornell Maritime Press, New York, 1943.

Kotsch, William, *Weather for the Mariner,* Naval Institute Press, Annapolis, MD, 1983.

Petterssen, Sverre, *Introduction to Meteorolgy,* McGraw-Hill, New York, 1969.

Riehl, H., *Tropical Meteorology,* McGraw-Hill, New York, 1954.

———.*Sailing Directions for the North Pacific Ocean,* Defense Mapping Agency, Hydrographic Center, 1972.

———.*Sailing Directions for the West Coasts of Mexico and Central America,* Defense Mapping Agency, Hydrographic Center, 1990.

———.*U.S. Navy Marine Climatic Atlas of the World, Vol. II North Pacific Ocean,* Naval Weather Service Detachment, Asheville, NC, 1977.

———.*World Wide Marine Weather Broadcasts,* National Oceanic and Atmospheric Administration, 1993.

Index

Appendices

Appendices

Appendices

Appendices

Numerals & Symbols

Appendices

Order Form

Please send me the following books, inscribed by the authors:

* *MexWX: Mexico Weather for Boaters*
  Capt. John E. Rains $19.95
* *Cruising Ports: Florida to California via Panama*
  Capt. John E. Rains $22.95
* *Boating Guide to Mexico: West Coast Edition*
  Capts. John E. Rains & Patricia Miller $39.95

Name _____

Street _____

City & State _____

ZIP _____

For California addresses only, include the following sales tax:
  MexWX   *add $1.55   ($21.50)*
  Cruising Ports   *add $1.78   ($24.74)*
  Boating Guide to Mexico   *add $3.10   ($43.05)*

Shipping: US PS Book Rate: $2.25 for first book
        $1 for each additional book (Allow 7 to 14 days)
Priority Mail: $3.50 for first book
        $2 for each additional book (Allow 3 to 5 days)

Send check or money order payable to:
Point Loma Publishing   **Amount of Check $ _____**
P.O. Box 60190
San Diego, CA 92166

ᴜᴜᴜᴜᴜᴜᴜᴜᴜᴜᴜᴜᴜᴜᴜᴜᴜᴜᴜᴜᴜᴜ

Credit Card Orders -------------- or toll free: (888) 302-2628
Name on card _____ **Visa/MC/other**
Card Number _____ **Exp date** _____
Daytime Phone _____

For yacht delivery and trip consulting inquiries, please contact
          Captain John E. Rains
(619) 222-9028   **email: www.inetworld.net/rains**